Through the Year with
Songs of Praise

For the camera, lighting and sound crews of the BBC Outside Broadcast teams

Text Acknowledgments

Every effort has been made to trace the relevant text and picture copyright holders. We apologize for any inadvertent omissions or errors, and ask those concerned to contact the publishers, who will ensure that full acknowledgment is made in the future.

Scripture quotations except where noted are taken from the Revised English Bible with the Apocrypha copyright © 1989 by Oxford University Press and Cambridge University Press.

Scripture on p. 180 taken from the Authorized Version of the Bible (The King James Bible), the rights in which are vested in the Crown, are reproduced by permission of the Crown's Patentee, Cambridge University Press.

p. 36 Prayer by Janet Morley from *All Desires Known*. Copyright © Janet Morley. Published by SPCK.

pp. 74–75 *The Bird of Heaven* by Sydney Carter, copyright © 1969 Stainer & Bell Ltd and p. 76 *Lord of the Dance* by Sydney Carter, copyright © 1963 Stainer & Bell Ltd, PO Box 110, Victoria House, 23 Gruneisen Road, London N3 1DZ.

p. 85 'Walk with me, O my Lord' by Estelle White. Copyright © McCrimmon Publishing Company Ltd.

p. 88 'In the Lord I'll be ever thankful' copyright © Ateliers et Presses de Taizé, 71250 Taizé-Community, France.

p. 95 'The Swallow Poem' from *The Swallow Book* by Ernst Toller, edited by Ashley Dukes (translator), 1924. Used by permission of Oxford University Press.

p. 115 'Spirit of God' copyright © R.T. Brooks. Used by permission of Oxford University Press.

p. 148 'Remember Him' copyright © Sir Christopher Foxley-Norris. Reproduced by kind permission of Lady Foxley-Norris.

pp. 162–63 'A Hymn for Remembrance Sunday' by Fred Kaan. Copyright © 1997 Stainer & Bell Ltd, PO Box 110, Victoria House, 23 Gruneisen Road, London N3 1DZ.

p. 167 'Jesus the Lord said', an Urdu hymn translated by C.D. Monaghan. Copyright © Trustees for Methodist Church Purposes. Used by permission of Methodist Publishing House.

p. 172 Text of 'Tell out, my soul' copyright © Timothy Dudley-Smith and used by permission.

p. 186 'BC:AD' copyright © U.A. Fanthorpe, *Christmas Poems*, 2002. Reproduced by permission of Peterloo Poets.

p. 192 'Let there be peace on earth', words & music by Sy Miller & Jill Jackson © copyright 1956 Jan Lee Music, USA. Cyril Shane Music Limited. All rights reserved. International copyright secured.

Picture Acknowledgments

All images © Andrew Barr, except where noted below.

pp. 11, 45 (top), 55, 83, 107 and 149 copyright © Lion Hudson.

p. 27 'Girl with yellow star (self portrait)'. Copyright © Marianne Grant. Reproduced from *I Knew I Was Painting for My Life: The Holocaust artworks of Marianne Grant*, edited by Deborah Haase and Ellen McAdam, published April 2002 by Glasgow Museums, Kelvingrove Art Gallery and Museum, Glasgow G3 8AG. With thanks to Marianne Grant and Deborah Haase for their assistance.

p. 96 Caricature by Emilio Coia.

p. 104 Photograph taken by Daisy Hayes.

p. 172 Sculpture *Virgin and Child* (1974) by Josephina de Vas Concellos, photographed by Andrew Barr at Blackburn Cathedral.

Picture research on the following pages courtesy of Zooid Pictures Limited: pp. 64 Todd Stone/AP Photo, 76 Redferns Music Picture Library, 103 and 164 Hulton|Archive/Getty Images, 110 Torleif Svensson/Corbis UK Ltd, 121 Rob Rayworth/Alamy, 159 Chris Balcombe/Rex Features, 166 Roger-Viollet/Rex Features, 171 Leslie Garland/Leslie Garland Picture Library/Alamy.

Contents

● ●

Foreword

• • • • • • • • • • • • • •

As a child, music was incredibly important to me. This is something that has not changed as time has gone by. Now, as an adult, it still has a central place in my life. I would not be able to exist without it.

I am fortunate, for some years, to have been one of the main presenters of BBC ONE's *Songs of Praise*. As far as I'm concerned it really is a dream job. I get to visit many of the world's greatest churches and cathedrals – I even get to sing in quite a few of them!

As well as the hymns and music, which you would expect me to love, it is also a wonderful, humbling experience to meet so many different people who have stories that are often very moving.

In this book we find many such stories, Andrew's own rich memories and some of the behind-the-scenes moments from programmes. If anybody knows about *Songs of Praise,* that person is Andrew; he has an infectious enthusiasm for the programme and a playful air about him. It is no wonder then that we get on like a house on fire, and spend many an outside broadcast recording in each other's company.

These stories in Andrew's book are linked to days or seasons through the year, but it is a book that is lovely to dip into at any time.

I, of course, have my own memories of individuals and of places, and some of these are echoed here. However, this book draws on a treasure-trove of experience of the programme, stretching over more than 40 years. Andrew brings to the reader a warmth and a depth of feeling for the people he describes and the stories that he tells. I thoroughly enjoyed reading this book and am sure that it will bring pleasure to many people as they read it throughout the year.

Aled Jones

Preface

● ● ● ● ● ● ● ● ● ● ● ● ● ● ●

I cannot remember much about the first *Songs of Praise* I ever watched, but I think it must have been on an autumn Sunday in the 1960s, soon after the very first programme went out from a Baptist chapel in Cardiff. I was staying with a school friend, Christopher, on the south coast of England, where television reception (still in black and white) was decidedly erratic and subject to snowstorms every time a car drove by or there was thunder in the air. But arriving from a TV-less home, I was soon hooked on Christopher's weekend TV routine of Saturday night with *Dixon of Dock Green* and Sunday night with *Songs of Praise*. A transmission from a large parish church with hymns sung in the setting of high Anglican trappings encouraged Christopher, who had once been a promising treble under Sir William McKie at Westminster Abbey, into a display of 'air organ', the organist's equivalent of air guitar. Our TV supper table was imperilled by his wildly gyrating arms, reliving Sir William's flamboyant playing, all stops out and feet flying across imaginary pedals for the final hymn; and even I, a complete non-singer, found myself singing along with *Songs of Praise*.

This companion to a programme which is still going strong after 40 years, reflects the addiction which I share with five million regular viewers in Britain alone, and many more around the world. Following the Christmas and Easter companions, this book travels through a whole year with *Songs of Praise*. Here are current behind-the-scenes stories of a TV programme that for 32 years I helped make, both as director and producer and for a time as the series editor. And here too are the

inspiring stories at the heart of every programme, which have helped make the journey of faith a little clearer for me and for many others who watch each Sunday. I have also included some of our best-loved hymns and songs which did not quite make it into the top 40 of the Nation's Favourite Hymns.

This companion begins at the start of the New Year in January, but I hope that it will be just as enjoyable to open it and begin at your favourite time of the year. I have included the big stories of the Christian year, which the church begins to tell in December. We follow the natural seasons, and find out how the producers of *Songs of Praise* celebrate spring and harvest, and how they cope with a complex schedule which sometimes means that the recording of a Palm Sunday programme may have to take place at Christmas.

With ten thousand saints listed in the latest guide, your own favourite may well be missing, and as there are more than a hundred special Sundays for different churches each year, I can't even begin to do justice to this rich diversity. But I have tried to capture, as far as I can, how the changing seasons can affect us all. We all have our own view of when the seasons begin and end, and the church's year is set by the date of Easter, so the chronology in this book is inevitably rather approximate and is intended as a rough guideline only.

Much of the enjoyment of writing this book has come from the generous help so many have offered whenever *Songs of Praise* is mentioned. The programme has opened many doors. In particular, as I wandered about Louth in Lincolnshire, Conrad Wilson came out and helped me clamber up onto the roof of his house to show me the best position to photograph Louth's fine parish church, which has, so it is said, the tallest spire in England. As we both clung to the TV aerial on his chimney pot, I realized that only loyalty to the series could have induced someone to climb onto their own roof on one of the hottest summer afternoons of the year, to help a passing stranger with a camera. The result is a view that I have never seen before – obviously – and one which eluded the BBC nearly 35 years ago when I was there as part of the *Songs of Praise* production team for the very first time.

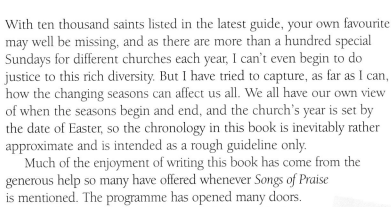

Once again I am indebted to Morag Reeve, Nick Rous and Olwen Turchetta at Lion Hudson for much editorial support and imaginative design, and to my long-suffering friends in the current *Songs of Praise* team, headed by Hugh Faupel and Michael Wakelin, who allow me to spy on them and ask them innumerable questions while they work. Kathleen Frew, who first learnt to decipher my handwriting in BBC Scotland, now produces word-perfect translations of my jottings made on journeys that form the starting point of this book. Liz, my wife, has, as ever, made the difference, not only in detecting the dreaded 'waffle viruses', but in bringing her wisdom and knowledge to my ideas and travelling with me through the year.

In the 1950s, before I was given a Box Brownie camera for Christmas, I used to draw tiny pictures of Britain packed with intricate detail, scarcely intelligible to anyone but me. Many years have gone by since we took family walks under the North Downs in the Shoreham valley, where some of my own drawings were inspired, and I have now come across the almost mystical engravings of the nineteenth-century artist, Samuel Palmer. He achieved with great beauty the effects I had been striving for but lacked the skill to achieve. However, the landscapes he drew, he wrote, are only a beginning:

Landscape is of little value, but as it hints or expresses the haunts and doings of man. However gorgeous, it can be but Paradise without an Adam. Take away its churches, where for centuries the pure word of God has been read to the poor in their mother tongue, and in many of them most faithfully preached to the poor, and you have a frightful kind of Paradise left – a Paradise without God.

The same can be said of the beautiful portraits of our countryside that nature programmes on television show us today. And that is why, although in my BBC career I worked on many other types of programme, it was the one that first introduced me to the joys of television, *Songs of Praise*, with its stories of human faith expressed in hymns and songs sung in churches old and new at the heart of all our changing landscapes, that became my companion through the years. I hope that you will join me on the journey.

Through all the changing scenes of life,
in trouble and in joy,
the praises of my God shall still
my heart and tongue employ.
N. TATE (1652–1715) AND N. BRADY (1659–1726)

WINTER:

JANUARY TO MARCH

Another Time, Another Way

• • • • • • • • • • • • •

NEW YEAR

'Yes, of course, if it's fine tomorrow,' said Mrs Ramsay.
'But you'll have to be up with the lark,' she added.

To her son these words conveyed an extraordinary joy,
as if it were settled the expedition were bound to take
place, and the wonder to which he had looked forward,
for years and years it seemed, was, after a night's
darkness and a day's sail, within touch.

'But,' said his father, stopping in front of the drawing-
room window, 'it won't be fine.'

FROM *TO THE LIGHTHOUSE* BY VIRGINIA WOOLF (1882–1941)

'We'll do it,' my own father used to say to any request to visit and
explore a new place and then, after a pause just long enough to
ensure that his two sons were attending, 'another time.' It was a ritual
in our home life, especially at the beginning of a new year, when in the
aftermath of Christmas my brother and I would be full of plans and schemes
for the year ahead. We could keep on hoping, since we always knew that he
meant to keep his promise, but, like Mr Ramsay, our father's demeanour
was always so gloomily pessimistic that he gave us the impression that
nothing was at all certain. Anticipation kept us going through dark winter
afternoons until eventually, the following Easter, or summer or autumn, we
would usually go. But even now, 50 years on, the most magical journey can
never quite fulfil the promise of hours and days and weeks spent dreaming
about it.

Nothing can have seemed more important to my mother and father, along
with so many of their generation, than bringing up their children in safety
after a terrifying war, which for the first time had brought an enemy into the
skies above every home. I have only vague memories of wartime and as a

child could not understand why thunderstorms and sudden power cuts left survivors of the Blitz untroubled. To them it was enough that a daily cycle of birdsong and distant church bells had taken over again from air-raid warnings, anti-aircraft guns and the murderous detonation of flying bombs. Beyond one of the big trees that marked a limited horizon from my bedroom window, an entire family had been killed in April 1941. After the war, bomb sites were a familiar feature of Sunday afternoon walks, and good places to find the wild flowers that had to be pressed in a book for 'nature study' lessons at school. These were the early days in post-war England when the older generation quietly and thankfully celebrated the peace.

Most days of the year are what the church calls 'days in ordinary time'. Sometimes in winter, simply overwhelmed with impatience for something to happen, I would try to escape from 'ordinary time' into a private world, by creating a sun-filled summer mountain or an imaginary city on a piece of drawing paper. The 'high' days of Easter, summer and Christmas seemed to come agonizingly slowly over the distant horizon, and there were months and months of routine to live through before we could hope to arrive at the fulfilment of my father's promised 'another time'.

Meanwhile the seasons of the year, and the moments that marked out one week or month from another, sometimes provided other occasions to celebrate. I decorated an old diary with luridly crayoned bunting to mark the queen's coronation in June 1953, and I even anticipated the birthday of an extremely unreliable cleaner that month with exploding colour rockets.

In the final days before the queen's coronation, my father initiated a daily ceremony to mark what we thought of as a new age of 'young Elizabethans'. He unearthed an old flagpole and Union Jack from a dark corner of the attic and erected them in the front garden. My brother's and my offering of a row of moth-eaten flags from the toy box (including that of Imperial Japan) was rejected in favour of yards of new, brightly coloured bunting, which he festooned across the front of the house.

My father now rose even earlier than the usual two hours he required to prepare before leaving for work. Each morning at first light the Union Jack was solemnly hoisted, declaring to the empty avenue that our loyal household was en fête. At dusk, the procedure was reversed. Unfortunately the days were entirely windless and increasingly damp. Our flag could not be coaxed into even a small flutter. On 2 June, coronation day itself, we celebrated in a way that probably broke an ancient law. My father flew a different flag, the Lion Rampant of Scotland; but it, too, clung gloomily to the flagpole as steady rain set in.

Indoors, we listened in devout silence to 'All people that on earth do dwell' on the radio broadcast from Westminster Abbey and stood each time 'God Save the Queen' was played. By the end of the day, my father was convinced that our festive display was attracting a rain god. Next day, we reverted to 'ordinary time' and pole and flags vanished. And I seem to remember that as the world went back to work, the summer weather returned.

Another New Year, and in late middle age I am still planning hopeful journeys for the months ahead. The son of a pessimist must surely try to be an optimist, but I realize that I have inherited many of my late father's ways, and sometimes I even catch myself promising myself to go somewhere 'another time'. But this year has actually begun with a visit long ago promised for 'another time', but one that we never actually achieved together in his lifetime.

I am travelling north, my favourite direction, along the old Fosse Way. On this ancient route, older even than a Roman road, it is easy to imagine my father 'taking quietly' as he used to describe a journey by car – driving steadily but rather slowly. This long, straight road is the sort he most enjoyed. He would sit very upright and still on the front bench seat of our Ford Consul, the ash of the perennial cigarette drooping longer and longer but miraculously never falling, until snatched away by my mother, who could no longer bear the suspense.

I can easily see why he liked this particular road, for it is part of a quiet route that links the West Country with the Midlands, without a motorway in sight. You seem to be taken by stealth along a secret, ancient route through the back garden of England. At a crossroads there may be a brief encounter with one of the Cotswolds' major tourist routes, but soon you are alone again on the old, straight road.

A small roadside sign to Sapperton tempts me off the way. This was the place I first longed to visit years ago. On this January day I don't have to hurry to get home to Scotland, and all these years later, I have come here at last. I drive down a long, muddy track leading to the Tunnel House inn, for nearby is one of the great engineering feats of the Industrial Revolution: the mysterious ornamental mouth of the old canal tunnel at Sapperton. In January, the bare branches of Gloucestershire woodland cannot conceal the now long-forgotten canal, whose water is scarcely ankle deep. It is a melancholy sight, but there is exciting news in the inn that enthusiasts have made a New Year resolution to restore the once great waterway.

The tunnel was blasted through the high Cotswold ridge to link the River Thames and the River Severn through the Cotswolds. It was so important that King George III came to open it on 19 November 1789. In Temple Thurston's classic book *The Flower of Gloster*, the author described an Edwardian journey by barge through the ornamental arch into the darkness of Sapperton Tunnel under the inn. Together with an old bargeman from nearby Eynsham, he used the side walls of the tunnel to literally haul the heavy boat through the tunnel, a traditional skill called 'legging'.

For four hours Eynsham Harry and I lay upon our sides on the wings that are fitted to the boat for that purpose, and legged every inch of the two and three-quarter miles. It is no gentle job. Countless were the number of times I looked on ahead to that faint pin-point of light; but by such infinite degrees did it grow larger as we neared the end, that I thought we should never reach it.

Temple Thurston's description of the journey through the tunnel seems to exactly match those hours of anticipation I spent as a child in the long, dark days of winter, waiting for 'another time'.

As Thurston set out on his canal voyage before the First World War, he urged his readers to join him in the spirit of discovery.

… not merely that setting of one's prow towards the far horizon of the unknown – that is the spirit of adventure. The spirit of discovery lies in the eye and the mind. He whose sight is young enough to find anew the world that has been found by others, he is the discoverer, and, by right of that power of which he holds the secret, a man may reveal new worlds wherever he goes.

Reading Thurston again, at the end of my New Year visit to the old canal tunnel, I think I can also see another way of understanding my father and his

mournful refrain of 'another time'. He wasn't being an eternal pessimist. For him the pace of life, bringing up two impatient boys, needed to be kept slow and steady. As he searched and found regular work after his war service in the army, he 'legged' us through 'ordinary time', looking ahead to the distant pinprick of light of the sunny days to come, and making sure we held on to our hopes and spirit of discovery. It would be a long, slow slog ahead for us all.

Thurston described how Eynsham Harry and he finally emerged into Golden Valley.

It was evening when we came out into the light again and, though the sun had set, with shadows falling everywhere, it almost dazzled me.

I remember childhood January afternoons when, as a final treat before school began again, we were taken to the news cinema at Victoria Station in London. Here we forgot boring routine and feasted our eyes on the brilliantly coloured Disney cartoons that, interspersed with the drama of British Movietone News, were on continuous show. After all too short a time it seemed, my mother would stand up again whispering, 'This is where we came in.'

For a short while we had imagined that we were out of the tunnel and in Golden Valley. Now it was time to get back to the natural rhythm of ordinary time at home and in school, making something of our journey 'legging' through the seasons.

The last time I saw my father was just before he died. He was still promising 'another time'.

'When the spring comes,' he said, lying in his hospital bed, 'we'll have a walk together in a field of daffodils.'

During his funeral a few weeks later in February, as we were singing one of his favourite hymns, I looked out through the plain glass of the chapel windows to see the first daffodils opening up on the slopes of Salisbury Plain.

Forth in thy name, O Lord, I go,
my daily labour to pursue;
thee, only thee, resolved to know
in all I think or speak or do.

The task thy wisdom hath assigned
O let me cheerfully fulfil;
in all my works thy presence find,
and prove thy good and perfect will.

Thee may I set at my right hand,
whose eyes my inmost substance see,
and labour on at thy command,
and offer all my works to thee.

Give me to bear thy easy yoke,
and every moment watch and pray,
and still to things eternal look,
and hasten to thy glorious day;

for thee delightfully employ
whate'er thy bounteous grace hath given,
and run my course with even joy,
and closely walk with thee to heaven.

CHARLES WESLEY (1707–88), ALTD

Epiphany in the Video Cupboard

EPIPHANY

Three kings from Persian lands afar
To Jordan follow the pointing star:
And this the quest of the travellers three,
Where the new-born King of the Jews may be.
Full royal gifts they bear for the King;
Gold, incense, myrrh are their offering.

The star shines out with a steadfast ray;
The Kings to Bethlehem make their way,
And there in worship they bend the knee,
As Mary's child in her lap they see;
Their royal gifts they show to the King;
Gold, incense, myrrh are their offering.

Thou child of man, lo, to Bethlehem
The kings are travelling, travel with them!
The star of mercy, the star of grace,
Shall lead thy heart to its resting-place.
Gold, incense, myrrh thou canst not bring,
Offer thy heart to the infant King,
Offer thy heart!

THE THREE KINGS BY PETER CORNELIUS (1824–74)

There is one New Year resolution that I know that I could never make, let alone keep, which is to invite the *Life Laundry* into our home. It's a programme I watch from behind the sofa, shuddering with sympathy for the victim's predicament as almost all their possessions are laid out on huge squares in their garden and then, while some are wheeled out to a car boot sale, the rest wait to be fed into the mouth of a large shredder that is wheeled in. This drastic clear-out is intended to transform mind, body and soul and free the people to make a fresh start. By the end of the programme, each week's victim is left in a home with acres of newly revealed space, and all the bursting cupboards and untidy piles of old familiar objects which might 'come in useful some day' have been replaced by a handful of banknotes. So life can begin.

Not in our house. No thank you!

My *Songs of Praise* memory bank overflows out of a large cupboard that would be just right for the *Life Laundry* team to hang their coats. The cupboard houses my collection of video recordings of television programmes from the past thirty years, once beautifully sorted and indexed by my wife Liz, but now muddled both by me and by a succession of bored pets who have nipped in when the door was open and concluded their own examination by triggering an avalanche of tapes. Now I alone can make any sense of this chaos.

The boxes are old and dusty, labels have almost peeled off, but none of that matters when a treasured *Songs of Praise* tape from long ago suddenly comes back to life in the video player. To start a New Year rooting around in this cupboard has for me all the surprise and pleasure of unopened Christmas parcels. I was looking for Sally Magnusson's recent 2004 *Songs of Praise* on the theme of gifts, but instead I found a box marked with fading hieroglyphics, concealing the Epiphany *Songs of Praise* from 1985. Cliff Michelmore, standing in front of Liverpool's Roman Catholic Cathedral, has unexpectedly and pleasurably suddenly come to light.

When in the 1960s the late Sir Frederick Gibberd designed his curious wigwam-shaped building in Liverpool, I wonder whether he realized that the resonant acoustic which he had created would give even the least able singer the confidence to join in the hymns in praise of God. In 1985, for the Epiphany *Songs of Praise*, a huge choir produced an exciting sound to celebrate the arrival of the wise men. There were plenty of young voices too, fulfilling the hope expressed by Cardinal Heenan in a letter sent to the architect in 1959:

The priests and people of the archdiocese of Liverpool will beg God to enlighten you. You will also have the powerful prayers of our children. It is for them and their children's children that you will build.

As ever in *Songs of Praise*, it was people with no claim to celebrity whose stories of faith were the gifts of gold, frankincense and myrrh, although one of the contributors, Bob Paisley, then manager of Liverpool Football Club, was at least a local hero. He told Cliff that the football team was a great ambassador for the city, dispelling the ugly image created by the inner-city riots of 1981.

Two of the city's own 'wise men' revealed their New Year resolution for revitalizing the life of the people of Liverpool. With his friend, the Anglican Bishop David Sheppard, the Roman Catholic Archbishop, Derek Worlock, looked out across the city. 'We have great assets here,' he said. 'Some see only the dirty old Mersey, but it is in fact a fine river. We must develop its tourist potential.'

David Sheppard said, 'We've got to try to renew our community both spiritually and materially. Our whole Christian concern isn't just expressed in preaching, but in living a life alongside people.'

Since then *Songs of Praise* has been back to Liverpool many times, including a celebration of the Festival of the Sea, held among the tourist attractions of the cleaned up old Albert Dock that the two church leaders had worked for. A familiar old landscape had been seen in a new way and it led to transformation.

Watching the Liverpool Cathedral Choir singing Peter Cornelius's *Three Kings* has triggered my mind back to a yearly New Year treat when we lived in Kent. Well into his eighties, Len, a member of our small church choir, retained a pure tenor voice and always sang *The Three Kings* as a solo, as his Epiphany gift to the church. At no other time in the year did we in the congregation sit so quiet and still.

I wonder about those original three wise men. Who were they? And what significance can they have for me or anyone else today? When I made a film once, asking people who they thought they were, the Church of England had not yet suggested, as it did in 2004, that they could in fact have been women. For my film we recorded a batch of vox pops, those familiar interviews with people in the street. There was a lot of confusion but the consensus seemed to be that they were rich and 'well-read', and one man insisted that there had been four, not three. I don't think anyone could remember their traditional names, and I've had to look them up again myself.

The film went on to meet some of Britain's five thousand followers of the Zoroastrian religion, who claim descent from the learned people of what in biblical times was the Persian empire, part of which bordered the Holy Land. At the heart of lives devoted to prayer and charity is a reverence for fire as a symbol of purity. In the last century, funnily enough, three eminent

Zoroastrians became MPs, one Conservative, one Labour and one Liberal. But my film, made in a North London house during a fire ceremony celebrating a silver wedding anniversary, probably did little to help solve the mystery of the origins of Caspar, Melchior and Balthazar.

However, in the first few days of this New Year, I suddenly began to remember when three wise men had appeared in my own life. Thinking about my first headmaster, who had just died in his 92nd year, reminded me of his scripture lessons and his enthusiasm for the three wise men. The familiar carol, 'We three kings of orient are', was even sung at his funeral. Major Hodges would often test us to see whether we could recall their exotic names. A former adjutant in the Royal Tank Regiment, he had a mischievous sense of humour. Anyone dropping off in his class would come to with a start when a discreetly inflated paper bag was exploded behind their head, without further rebuke.

I remember Major Hodges as gifted and wise but also as eccentric a headmaster as any enquiring mind could hope for, and he recruited two equally unusual military colleagues from the backwash of wartime England. I now see that they were indeed my own three wise men, imparting vital gifts to an immature mind. Captain Scott, who had served with Montgomery of Alamein, drilled into us the essentials of Latin and an understanding of language. To help us become what he called 'good grammarians' he led us through the dark events of *Caesar's Gallic Wars* and brought it so much to life that we felt we could easily have held a conversation with Julius Caesar. A lonely demeanour and a natural courtesy, which meant that his elegant threats of cataclysmic punishment for acts of mischief never quite rang true, ensured our undying loyalty to Captain Scott.

Some of us also followed the life and times of his colleague, Samuel Francis Braham, right up to his death years after we had all grown up. He was our 'Mr Chips', proud of his pioneering work with the Scout Movement and service in the Royal Sussex Regiment. Officially, he had the task of teaching us English, but really he was imparting basic intelligence. He never ever raised a hand in anger, but he ruled us with sudden outbursts of deafening rage, which vanished just as rapidly as they appeared. I can see him today, in his M.C.C. tie, wreathed in the pipe smoke that heralded a peaceful lesson. His own handwriting was worse than the proverbial doctor's, but valuing his praise we would go to great efforts to read his red annotations to our homework. He was particularly fond of rapidly dictating leaders from *The Times*, from which I developed the skill of quickly writing down verbatim conversations without recourse to shorthand – a skill that has served me well as a TV director. He would also invent awkward, old relatives coping with parlous emergencies, to help us develop letter-writing skills.

MR BRAHAM – MY 'MR CHIPS'

Like Captain Scott, Mr Braham cut rather a lonely figure and my brother and I were pleased when my mother once invited him to dinner at our home. Whereupon, he created a full-blown domestic emergency. In our quiet road, we spotted his lopsided gait far off as he approached – on completely the wrong night. A pantomime followed as my mother conjured up many courses from an empty larder, while my father was taught his lines by my brother on the way back, via a different route, from the evening train. Mr Braham's own thank you letter was a masterpiece combining courtesy with a growing suspicion of the truth.

Almost 50 years ago, these three teachers offered me their gifts of life-skills, which are still in daily use. None more than the intimations of immorality, the myrrh offered by the headmaster, as every weekday morning he read aloud from the *Book of Common Prayer*. Standing behind my desk unaware that here was a gift for me, I used to watch fascinated as with a silver propelling pencil he carefully traced his way through Cranmer's beautiful words. Years before their meaning sunk in, I knew the words by heart. More than once in tense moments just before a *Songs of Praise* recording, I have been able to hear again his voice in my head, praying the 'Collect for Grace', as well as the tips for survival he described as 'the three Ks': cool, calm and collected.

The headmaster's judgment was flawless in introducing us to Cranmer. But at the end of my New Year's day journey into the past in the lumber of the overflowing video cupboard, I realize that its chaotic contents probably also reveal my top wise man's occasional lapses of judgment – when he once awarded me the school 'neatness prize'. But perhaps my man in the street was right, and there were four wise men after all, and the fourth was bearing 'things that might one day come in useful'.

O Lord our heavenly Father, Almighty and everlasting God, who hast safely brought us to the beginning of this day; defend us in the same with thy mighty power; and grant that this day we fall into no sin, neither run into any kind of danger; but that all our doings may be ordered by thy governance, to do always that is righteous in thy sight; through Jesus Christ our Lord.

Amen

MORNING PRAYER, THE THIRD COLLECT FOR GRACE TO LIVE WELL,
FROM *THE BOOK OF COMMON PRAYER* BY THOMAS CRANMER

The Shepherds' Farewell

THE SECOND SUNDAY IN EPIPHANY

Thou must leave thy lowly dwelling, the humble crib, the stable bare.
Babe all mortal babes excelling, content our earthly lot to share,
Loving father, loving mother, shelter thee with tender care!
Blessed Jesus, we implore thee with humble love and holy fear,
In the land that lies before thee, forget not us who linger here!
May the shepherd's lowly calling ever to thy heart be dear!
Blest are ye beyond all measure, thou happy father, mother mild!
Guard ye well your heav'nly treasure, the Prince of Peace, the
    Holy Child!
God go with you, God protect you, guide you safely through the wild!

THE SHEPHERDS' FAREWELL BY HECTOR BERLIOZ (1803–69)

It is hard to imagine a more remarkable outcome of a dull social evening. In 1850, the 31-year-old French composer, Hector Berlioz, jotted down these words, while bored by his companions. He even sketched out a beautiful melody, which choirs now sing at Evensong during Epiphany. The chorus was to be the beginning of a full-length work, *The Childhood of Christ*, first performed in Paris at Christmastime in 1854.

The composer was in a highly emotional state, remembering the joy of his childhood faith that he feared he might be losing, although there seems no hint of loss in the words or serene music in this familiar classic. I remember an extraordinary moment in 1974, in a busy videotape editing area of the BBC Television Centre, always full of preoccupied technicians, when Ray Short, the first series editor of *Songs of Praise*, was making a final check on a tape of an Epiphany programme, which included *The Shepherds' Farewell* sung by the famous choir of St John's College, Cambridge, conducted by the legendary George Guest. The entire editing area fell absolutely quiet for a few moments, a kind of Epiphany in itself.

Burns' Night

● ● ● ● ● ● ● ● ● ● ● ● ●

25 JANUARY

Some have meat and cannot eat.
Some cannot eat that want it:
But we have meat and we can eat
Sae let the Lord be thankit.

THE KIRKCUDBRIGHT GRACE (ALSO KNOWN AS THE *SELKIRK GRACE*) BY ROBERT BURNS (1759–96)

Tonight, around the world, Scots people (and many others too) celebrate the 'immortal memory' of Scotland's bard, Robert Burns. In January 1995, *Songs of Praise* came from Dumfries, where the poet died in 1796. Townspeople there, members of one of the world's oldest Burns' Clubs, meeting in their 'Howff', the Globe Inn, entertained Sir Harry Secombe as their special guest at a traditional Burns' night supper, a simple meal of haggis, 'neeps and 'tatties – a reminder, especially in these days of the 'gourmet menu', of the needs of a hungry world.

The World Through Marianne's Eyes

27 JANUARY – HOLOCAUST MEMORIAL DAY
For God alone I wait silently;
my hope comes from him.
He alone is my rock of deliverance,
my strong tower, so that I am unshaken.

PSALM 62:5–6

Our BBC film crew is in the smart living room of a villa in a genteel suburb of Glasgow. Outside, there is a thick frost but the winter sun floods in to light up Marianne's kindly face and bright eyes. We are offered the warmest hospitality and attention, and now the time has come and, as we have asked, she will tell the story of a life in another world, another time, a world and a time that can only be called hell. Marianne is a survivor of Auschwitz, the death camp liberated on this day in 1945.

It is tempting to turn away or switch to another channel when a face on the TV screen is telling you a true and terrible story. On one of the first televised Holocaust Memorial days, *Songs of Praise* followed Mayer Bormsztyk as he returned to his village in Poland where, on one day in November 1942 every one of his family and friends were murdered. Supported by children and grandchildren, he struggled bravely but tearfully to tell the story of his tiny part, a survivor of one of the most evil times in the history of the world. For Mayer, it was important that for the sake of his family, and for future generations, the record should be kept.

'It is important that as a Christian, I face the reality of the Holocaust,' said Stephen Smith of the Beth Shalom Holocaust Centre in Nottinghamshire. 'Christian people should lead the way to take us all into the future.'

It is heartening that Christian and Jewish congregations united for one of the very earliest *Songs of Praise* programmes 40 years ago, and since then the programme has even come from synagogues, because the Jewish psalms are the earliest and greatest songs of praise. But it is very uncomfortable to read or watch programmes about the Holocaust.

In Glasgow, I cannot turn away from Marianne as she describes the events leading up to the moment when she came face-to-face with one of the most evil Nazis, Josef Mengele. She describes how, after surviving two years in the appalling Jewish ghetto, Theresienstadt, she travelled to Auschwitz. When her mother was ordered into the cattle wagon transport, Marianne would not let her go on her own and although she herself was not on the list, managed to push her way onto the same train. Although in separate compartments, they both survived a journey on which many others died. While many more were gassed as soon as they left the train, Marianne and her mother later, miraculously, found each other in the enormous death camp. Marianne's story of devotion to her mother reminded me of the biblical story of Ruth and Naomi:

'Where you go, I shall go, and where you stay, I shall stay. Your people will be my people, and your God my God. Where you die, I shall die, and there be buried.'
RUTH 1:16–17

Marianne was to face another danger after the camp's guards discovered that the 23-year-old was a gifted artist, and she was put to work painting to entertain the children in the so-called 'family camp'. Her fame spread and one day a small boy came running to her, 'Painter, painter. Mengele wants you!'

'So I ran with him,' Marianne told me, 'you couldn't walk when Mengele wanted you – you had to run.'

Strutting up and down on a Persian carpet, something so beautiful in the middle of this dreadful place, Mengele watched closely as Marianne was ordered to make a drawing of young women twins. He never spoke to her. At another occasion she was given an architect's toolset of a sort that she had never used, and ordered to draw a complex family tree of a Hungarian dwarf family.

'I knew that if I had made a blob, that was me finished then and there,' Marianne tells us, adding in an almost matter of fact way, 'I really was painting for my life.'

Marianne only weeps when she remembers the children, one and a half million innocents murdered as part of Hitler's 'final solution'. But then this survivor of hell says, 'You have to have forgiveness in your heart. If you haven't got forgiveness in your heart, you're not a good person.'

Marianne is now in her 80s. She makes it easy for us to listen to her, for as she talks she brings in moments of wry humour, a characteristic of Jewish culture. She ends our interview with the reason why, for her, remembering and telling this awful story more than 50 years later is still worthwhile. She wants us to remember her story, so that we never forget how quickly ordinary men and women can be gripped by almost uncontrollable evil.

'Try and keep peace, wherever you are, whether it is family peace or to prevent any war. The young people suffer, the children suffer – and you can't recover from a war for a long, long, long time.'

There is something else that needs to be done, if we are not always to turn away in horror every time the faded film shots of this dreadful time of genocide are shown on TV. We must follow Marianne's lead in learning to forgive. For her, a survivor of hell, it must take a daily conscious decision. Having seen the look in her eyes, I know that this is what I too must learn to do – to forgive and never forget.

The God of Abraham praise,
at whose supreme command
from earth I rise and seek the joys
at his right hand.
I all on earth forsake,
its wisdom, fame and power;
and him my only portion make,
my shield and tower.

THOMAS OLIVERS (1725–99), PARAPHRASED FROM THE HEBREW *YIGDAL*

To Iona with T.L.C.

● ● ● ● ● ● ● ● ● ● ● ● ●

13 FEBRUARY

These are the words of the Lord: Take your stand and watch at the crossroads; enquire about the ancient paths; ask which is the way that leads to what is good. Take that way, and you will find rest for yourselves. But they said, 'We refuse.'

JEREMIAH 6:16

At 3 a.m., the wind redoubled its fury, huge blasts crashing against the old walls of the abbey outside my window. It was one of those nights when mere survival comes before sleep, and since my room in the B & B was apparently constructed from cardboard, the raw cold had necessitated desperate measures, and my narrow bed was twisted so that I could keep my toes inches from a tiny electric fire on the wall. After that I could only lie rigid, trying to compose an appropriate prayer before being blown away. The other big issue on my mind was what would happen not merely to my feet if the power failed, but to the 'live' BBC ONE broadcast that was scheduled to come from the abbey just a few hours from now? Why on earth had I taken such a risk?

I need not have been so anxious. I had reckoned without the wisdom of architects inspired first by the arrival of the hardy St Columba on Iona fourteen hundred years before, and then by one of the most remarkable and redoubtable Christians of the twentieth century, George MacLeod. With the examples of two such men, and designed to survive in one of Scotland's wildest places, the Abbey of Iona is not a house built on sand. Set in the spectacular surroundings of the Inner Hebrides, it has long been a popular *Songs of Praise* summer location; but I think that in February 1994, *This is the Day*, the rather less long-running Sunday morning programme which included viewers' prayers, was the first live broadcast to be attempted from the island during the short, storm-battered days of winter.

Iona is often described as 'a long way from anywhere', a description that will be met by the firm response that – from the islanders' point of view – so is London. Yet even from mainland Scotland you have to travel a long and ancient route to get to Iona, and for the last stage of your journey, you must go on foot. There are no convenient airports with car-rental booths to entice the unadventurous armchair traveller into action.

The wind was already frisky on the previous afternoon when our production team had boarded the little ferry that crosses the Sound of Iona from Mull. In the darkness, the vessel pitched and tossed towards a distant scattering of dim lights, our final destination. A taped safety message, which seemed more alarming than reassuring, was played over the ferry's tannoy.

'We're being done good,' I muttered through clenched teeth, 'following in the steps of St Columba.' My words were lost in the wind. A sea of green faces and forced smiles huddled around me stopped me from asking if anyone could remember the words of Godfrey Thring's hymn 'Fierce raged the tempest o'er the deep'.

At the top of a wet and treacherous slipway, shadowy figures with torches were waiting to greet us and guide us on foot to the abbey. Cars are not welcome on Iona, so we were all laden down with our bags, but arms were outstretched and there were embraces and handshakes in the dark as well as willing hands to help us unload our heavy and ungainly pieces of film equipment and to lead the way ahead. Deafened and battered by the wind, we stumbled along blindly after them in the dark, a motley BBC crew guided by our as yet unseen hosts, who had chosen to walk in the way of the saint who had died here 1,400 years before. We passed along the 700-year-old 'street of the dead', near the burial places of 48 Scots kings and where, not long after our programme was transmitted, John Smith, leader of the Labour Party, would be laid to rest. At last we were filing one at a time through a small door into warmth and light and a merciful quiet. No camels could ever be happier at making it through the eye of the needle.

For regular viewers of *This is the Day*, Iona was to be the end of a six-week pilgrimage from Glasgow, which had begun on Epiphany Sunday 1994. The presenter, Tony Phelan, was joined in each programme by three wise companions, Father Jim Byers, a Roman Catholic priest, Andy Redman, an artist from the Scottish Episcopalian Church and Kathy Galloway, the poet who has since become the Iona Community's first woman leader.

Although the abbey is an important place, the Iona Community itself is scattered all over the world, where its members live bound together by a Christian commitment to work and prayer and a simple lifestyle, with their headquarters in Govan, an inner-city district of Glasgow, where once their founder, George MacLeod, was the Church of Scotland minister. It was George MacLeod, both pacifist and war veteran, who 50 years before had first brought unemployed people to Iona to help complete the restoration of the abbey buildings and to start to draw hundreds of thousands of people to

what he called the 'thin place' – where little separated heaven from earth.

'You can't leave your own personal baggage behind when you come to Iona,' said Joanna Anderson, warden at the time of our broadcast. 'Uncomfortable experiences happen here. The beauty of places like Iona might appeal when times are hard, but our problems are not drowned in a sea of tranquillity.' In a corner of the abbey, we planned our broadcast in front of a huge multi-coloured net made by visitors from thousands of strands of wool, each representing an individual prayer. 'We're here to work and to be alongside people in all their difficulties,' said Joanna. It seemed a fitting symbol that this gentle place should be so buffeted by the winter storms outside.

If my own 'live' TV experience was a bit daunting, it was nothing to the Iona adventures of my predecessor, the pioneering religious broadcaster, the Reverend Dr Ronald 'Ronnie' Falconer. (Ronnie Falconer loved *Songs of Praise*, and over the first ten years of its life, probably produced more programmes than anyone else in its whole 40-year plus history.) As soon as he joined the BBC in the 1940s, he was determined to broadcast from Iona, even though there was then no electricity on the island. MacBrayne, the famous steamer company, refused to transport the acid-filled heavy-duty batteries that were needed in those days to transmit a radio programme. Undaunted, Ronnie made friends with fishermen based on the mainland in Oban, and each summer, his equipment was ferried around to the Iona slipway for a whole month of broadcasts.

In the 1950s, Ronnie set about making television programmes from the island, but now the fishermen could not help him, as no less than ten large vehicles were needed for a 'live' television broadcast. Enquiries were made to see if some of the West of Scotland's legendary 'puffers' could be chartered. The puffers, small steam coasters with flat bottoms allowing them to unload on remote beaches, were skippered by an eccentric generation of mariners immortalized by the writer Neil Munro in the stories of Para Handy and his decrepit vessel *The Vital Spark*.

In the end it was the War Office who provided the solution – in 1963 – when, after prolonged negotiations, a Tank Landing Craft, which normally supplied a rocket range in the Outer Hebrides, set sail from the Clyde on the 16-hour voyage, carrying 52 tons of BBC TV equipment. History does not record how the formidable pacifist George MacLeod felt about the full-scale military operation that allowed him to be seen and heard by TV viewers all around the world, but whatever he felt about it, the Army's T.L.C. beached to unload the BBC vans at Martyrs' Bay in the same way and on the same spot that Columba and his fellow monks had landed in AD 563.

Someone had the sense to make a film recording of the service that followed, but the huge, heavy, 2000-foot long 35 mm film rolls which have survived, each covering 20 minutes in black and white, are a far cry from the tiny digital cassettes that contain several hours of full-colour TV pictures today. The fragile contents of a pile of rusting film cans in the Scottish Film Archive are the only precious reminder of the 1963 day when, in spite of the inevitable stiff breeze, hundreds of visitors were able to disembark from MacBrayne's turbine steamer *King George V* and join George MacLeod in the sun for a televised service broadcast all over the world to mark the 1400th Anniversary of Columba's landing.

The programme began with a rare shot of the elegant but long-scrapped steamer at anchor in the sound of Iona, and then standing beneath the tall St Martin's Cross a huge crowd was revealed gathering around the community's founder.

'In the name of the whole church on this island of all churches, I greet you,' proclaimed George MacLeod in the familiar gravelly tone. 'I greet you from many lands and many denominations.' Watching the old black-and-white film years later, the viewer still feels greeted!

There are many of Ronnie Falconer's favourite off-the-cuff *Songs of Praise* shots of singers: two small boys peering from the back; a mother rocking a baby in her arms; young African students; and the inevitable kilts. A young priest, also at the back, takes a photo. I wonder what has become of him and his photograph of this historic broadcast.

George MacLeod preached with a huge, old Bible open in front of him. His text was from the Old Testament prophet Jeremiah and his voice echoed around the natural amphitheatre underneath the hill where Columba had once preached, as if he too had walked forward out of the ancient scripture.

'Ask for the old paths where there is the good way, and walk therein, and you will find rest for your souls.'

The preacher pointed to the old, paved way on which the pilgrims were standing, the same old road on which we were to stumble along in the darkness in February 1994:

'You have come like pilgrims here for over a thousand years to the shrine of St Columba. But if we are on a pilgrimage, it starts with a death. And we have to be buried with Christ in baptism if we are to rise to new life in him. What does it mean in Columba's terms to be committed to Christ? Have we to be committed to the past, a hopeless, romantic Celtic myth? No! It never meant that.'

George MacLeod went on to plead for a faith in God expressed through love of our neighbour and the struggle to build a just society, the central plank still of the Iona community. His prophecy for the third millennium 40 years before it began was:

'I sense we are on the edge of a new reformation. Christ is going to escape from the shrouds of misunderstanding.

Jeremiah wrote in a time when priests had gone off centre. Prophets were making false prophecies. And even now we are always looking for a religion in which we don't have to walk.'

He ended as the wind began to rise by reminding his worldwide audience of the pilgrims who had for centuries walked on the ancient way to Iona.

'Our dear ones who have gone forward ahead of us, died to the little hatreds, died to the greeds to rise again. They died before the work was finished, work not done by sword or tongue or pen. There is but one better way. Now it is for us to do.'

Thirty years on, Kathy Galloway picked up the theme of journeys on *This is the Day*. On that bleak February Sunday morning, the 'Way of the Dead' and the St Martin's Cross were deserted, but long after the death of George MacLeod, people are still coming to Iona, not just of different denominations now, but of different faiths, to look for common ground. Kathy said, 'It can be frightening to stand up; you stand out and you can become a target… you must take the risk to stand and leave safe ground to find common ground.'

At this point in our 1994 programme, the screen went blank. In the excitement of the 'live' broadcast, we had forgotten the vicious gale, but minutes from the end of the programme it blew our high-tech satellite dish off its essentially precise setting.

What followed is remembered by those of us who were there as 'the Iona miracle'. Normally the satellite dish can only be positioned in a lengthy specialist operation. In spite of the freezing gale, Andy, our satellite engineer, had remained standing loyally near the dish while we were on air, to stop it blowing away altogether. When it moved, he instinctively caught it and then simply leant on it. Defying all electronic and scientific logic, it immediately fell back into precisely the right position.

In less than a minute, we were back on the air for the final and strangely appropriate blessing, spoken by Joanna Anderson:

May the God who shakes heaven and earth,
whom death could not contain,
who lives to disturb and heal us,
bless us with power
to go forth and proclaim the gospel.
Amen.
JANET MORLEY

George MacLeod famously once said, 'If you believe in coincidences, I hope you have a very dull life.'

George Herbert

● ● ● ● ● ● ● ● ● ● ● ●

27 FEBRUARY
I travell'd on, seeing the hill, where lay my expectation.
FROM *THE PILGRIMAGE* BY GEORGE HERBERT (1593–1633)

This is the day when the Anglican Church remembers its most famous country vicar, George Herbert. If television had been invented in the seventeenth century, the story of this one man could have filled many episodes of a BBC TWO series following the progress of clergy life in rural parishes.

Born in 1593, Herbert came from an aristocratic Welsh family and at first, as a brilliant public orator of the University of Cambridge, had ambitions to be a favourite of King James I and the Royal Court. Then he suddenly renounced all worldly finery and retired to the country. In 1630 he became rector of the tiny country

ST MARY'S, LEIGHTON BROMSWOLD

parish of Bemerton, near Salisbury. Here 'Holy Mr Herbert', as he became known, turned from flowery oratory to writing some of England's finest poetry. Nowadays the profound simplicity of his verse is still greatly admired and sung in popular hymns, like 'Teach me, my God and King'.

In the winter of 1977, Mrs Dorothy Briggs, from another country parish, Godmanchester in Huntingdonshire, chose this hymn as she was filmed dusting and polishing the medieval parish church of St Mary, in the very first *Songs of Praise* in which interviews were included. 'Just treat it like your own home,' Mrs Briggs had been told when she had first taken on the work in 1950, 'just do half one week, and the other half the next week.' 'But of course, I do it *all* every week,' said Mrs Briggs. Her dedication to her 'common task' would have gladdened George Herbert's heart.

A mile or two to the west of Godmanchester is the prominent tower of St Mary's, Leighton Bromswold, all that survives of a brief career of George Herbert as a church architect. The poet was here in 1626, immediately after he had announced his 'resolution to enter into sacred orders' at the age of 33 and before he was given the living at Bemerton. Looking at his design, a spacious church dominated by an impressive but forbidding tower, to serve a tiny village, rather suggests that he may have spent more time waiting for the builders than on the cure of souls described in his later writing, *A Priest to the Temple, or, The Country Parson: His Character, and Rule of Holy Life*, in which he lays out his duties at home and abroad:

The Country Parson, when a just occasion calleth him out of Parish (which he diligently, and strictly weigheth, his Parish being all his joy and thought) leaveth not his Ministry behind him; but is himself where ever he is. Therefore those he meets on the way he blesseth audibly, and with those he overtakes or that overtake him, he begins good discourses, such as may edify, interposing sometimes short and honest refreshments, which may make his other discourses more welcome and less tedious.
FROM 'THE PARSON IN JOURNEY'

If Leighton Bromswold, with its single, broad, lawn-fringed street, was as beautiful in Herbert's time as it is now, he must have found it hard to leave – as I do today, after turning off the nearby A14 to visit it, pausing for some 'short and honest refreshments' on a long journey across England.

Teach me, my God and King,
in all things thee to see,
and what I do in anything
to do it as for thee.

A man that looks on glass
on it may stay his eye;
or if he pleaseth, through it pass,
and then the heaven espy.

All may of thee partake:
nothing can be so mean,
which, with this tincture, 'For thy sake',
will not grow bright and clean.

A servant with this clause
makes drudgery divine:
who sweeps a room, as for thy laws,
makes that and the action fine.

This is the famous stone
that turneth all to gold:
for that which God doth touch and own
cannot for less be told.
GEORGE HERBERT (1593–1633)

Owning Up

SHROVE TUESDAY

Forty days and forty nights
thou wast fasting in the wild,
forty days and forty nights
tempted and yet undefiled.

G.H. SMYTTAN (1822–70) AND FRANCIS POTT (1832–1909)

I confess to not being good at confessing. It's hard to 'own up', but Shrove Tuesday is the time not just for splurging on pancakes before Lent begins on Ash Wednesday but, by ancient tradition, it is the day for admitting the 'things done' and the 'things left undone' which mean, in the words of the old prayer book, 'there is no health in us.' The word 'shrove' is from an old English verb to 'shrive', originally meaning to impose a penance, but later coming to mean to make one's confession.

For some people, church is where they go to confess their sins to a priest. Although not a Roman Catholic, as a travel-stained visitor to London I sometimes drop in to Westminster Cathedral and sit at the back of the congregation at their week-day evening mass. Nearby are people at prayer, and many have come to make their confessions, which will be individually heard by a priest after the service.

It was as mass began one Lent evening a year ago that I heard a most beautiful voice close by. The singing of the distant choir at the far east end of the Cathedral was as mysterious and heavenly as always in this great building, but the solitary plaintive voice behind me seemed to be having an intense conversation with God. I could not turn round to see her without intruding, but as everyone went forward for communion, she passed me. She had the voice of an angel and the face of a child, but everything else seemed to have gone wrong for her physically, and clearly walking was a painful, agonizing process. As she struggled up towards the altar, there was no need for me to look up to the crucified figure on the great cross suspended above our heads, for an icon of innocent suffering.

When she returned, the solitary beautiful voice soared up again to heaven from amongst us mumbling commuters, and I imagined and prayed that her voice and her soul were setting her free from physical suffering. When I turned to leave, encumbered by my usual muddle of cases, carrier bags and unnecessary purchases, she was still at prayer, waiting for her turn to make her confession. She could not have known how much she had helped me begin my own.

Let us thine endurance share,
and awhile from joys abstain,
with thee watching unto prayer,
strong with thee to suffer pain.

'Forty days and forty nights'– 50 years ago, I stood to sing this hymn for the first time, the choir outnumbering the small congregation scattered about Beckenham parish church, and my father's low-pitched voice like an old but reliable car engine. The words of the hymn meant nothing to me. I was singing, as always, through clenched teeth, ever fearful that the vicar would make another kindly but misplaced attempt to corral me into the choir. I had the small boy's sin of always thinking everyone was looking at me.

It was 'Quadragesima', which the real world knows as the First Sunday in Lent. However, this was Prayer Book Matins, so it was Quadragesima and an elderly canon was standing in for the vicar as the 'officiant'. As a child, I was part of the 'faithful remnant' hearing a language that I knew well and yet whose meaning I had still to grasp.

I heard only the peaks and troughs, the sing-song rhythms and cadences of the old canon's voice preaching from and about a world that was clearly so holy he need have no fear of the 'prowling beasts'. I sat and counted the congregation. I reckoned that the canon must be feeling sad that so few of us have come to worship God with him. Not far away in London, thousands of people were packing into Harringay Stadium to hear Billy Graham.

Instead of listening to the sermon, I began planning single-handedly to start a revival in St George's, just to gladden the spirits of the old canon. I confess that this was some years before I realized that I was not in charge of the world.

And if Satan, vexing sore,
flesh or spirit should assail,
thou, his vanquisher before,
grant we may not faint nor fail.

Twenty years later I filmed a 15-year-old boy in nearby Chislehurst who really had started a religious revival in his school, and with evangelical fervour had turned the regular staid Morning Assembly into an impassioned rally that nobody wanted to miss. The education authorities were becoming a little alarmed. 'Where would it all lead?' they asked me. I don't know where it did

lead, but I confess that I identified with that boy's sense of mission.

I also confess that I myself had taken an easier route, and simply walked away from Matins and St George's, Beckenham. But recently, since seeing *Songs of Praise* coming from there, as well as a televised service on Whit Sunday, I went back to visit my old parish church. It has all been transformed.

The atmosphere today is warm and friendly, even on an ordinary weekday morning. There's no dust and no ancient canon to feel sorry for. Nobody tries to cajole you into joining the choir, since they are hugely proud of their singers who, under the direction of their organist, Nigel Groome, regularly feature on Radio 2's *Sunday Half Hour*, and have been heard on Radio 3's *Choral Evensong*. With its resonant acoustic, ideal for broadcasting, the church also offers a peaceful atmosphere of prayer for anyone who drops in.

There is always someone around who has time to listen – and I find I do want to talk. I want to tell them about the old days and own up that I had missed the point when I had sat in my pew worrying about the canon. My listener tactfully refrains from pointing out that I am rather older than she is, and she wasn't even born then. She shows me a sepia picture of the church as it was. I discover a trace of only one person from my time, the verger, commemorated in quite beautiful stained glass. My own memory is of a rather stern, disapproving presence as he conducted the old canon into church each Sunday.

The world has changed, and so has the weekday hospitality of so many churches, a thing almost unheard of in the 1950s. I have been part of that movement for change, and always searched out all things new. But I confess that today I am sometimes tempted to travel in the opposite direction. Even though I now have a responsibility for new liturgy in the Scottish Episcopal church, leading a small team who are writing new orders of service, I will drive for miles to attend Prayer Book Evensong, and even find beauty and inspiration in Matins.

I had forgotten my own youthful aversion to things old fashioned when I took our oldest grandson to church when he was ten. While the choir was singing a medieval anthem that I was finding unutterably beautiful, he whispered to me that he wanted a piece of paper. When I next looked at him, he was not drawing, as I had expected, but writing.

'This is…' was as far as I could read until he moved his hand and I saw the completed sentence '… boring.' He has never joined me in church again, since I resisted his implied request to leave at once.

If Lent is a time for owning up and penance, it is also a time for action. I mean to be more charitable about the difficult decisions facing the *Songs of Praise* production team this Lent, as they try to satisfy both my own, older generation, but also offer a musical celebration of faith for younger generations.

It would have been bizarre in the 1950s if clerics had announced that we would sing a hymn to the tune of Bill Haley and the Comets' hit: *Crazy, Man, Crazy* – a great favourite of mine in those days – or for churches to suddenly fill with coloured smoke or dry ice. But these things have become familiar features on *Songs of Praise*. These are not just the product of the desires of TV producers to 'do something original', they are a regular feature of worship in many of today's churches. Worship that makes use of new technology to visualize the timeless story is attracting the attention of the age group that sulked through Matins in the 1950s.

Songs of Praise tries to reflect what the churches call 'all-age worship'. They deploy the same state-of-the-art technology devices that are available to the pop-video producer. Aled Jones celebrated St David's Day by walking though a waterfall singing 'Jesu, lover of my soul', without getting wet. I watched a final edit of another programme with Michael Wakelin, current series producer of *Songs of Praise*, of Heather Small, the gospel singer, and Aled Jones wandering elegantly around candles on stands set in a disused railway shed.

In the edit suite, Garry Boon, the director, sat tensely motionless as his boss scrutinized his programme, peering closely at every shot, but increasingly gyrating about in his chair as the tempo heated up. After Heather Small's version of 'When a child is born', Michael called out, 'Now, I'm really boogieing!' But, curiously, his pleasure seemed complete when he heard the strains of a Hammond organ. I know Michael is no longer a teenager, but I had thought Hammond organs only belonged to my own musty old 1950s memories of Sandy McPherson on the BBC Theatre organ – but perhaps I need to show the tape to my grandson.

Meanwhile, I have no intention of giving up reading Thomas Cranmer's old Prayer Book this Lent. And I pray that I never forget the soul-searching sound of the young girl in Westminster Cathedral, singing so sweetly through her pain.

Keep, O keep us, Saviour dear,
ever constant by thy side;
that with thee we may appear
at the eternal Eastertide.
G.H. SMYTTAN (1822–70) AND FRANCIS POTT (1832–1909)

St David's Day

● ● ● ● ● ● ● ● ● ● ● ● ● ●

1 MARCH

… He brought the church into our homes,
put the holy vessels on the kitchen table
with bread from the pantry and wine from the cellar,
and he stood behind the table like a tramp
so as not to hide from us the wonder of the sacrifice.
And after the Communion we had a talk round the fire
and he spoke to us of God's natural order,
the person, the family, the nation and the society of nations,
and the Cross, which prevents us from making any one
of them into a god…

'THANKSGIVING PRAYER FOR ST DAVID', ANONYMOUS

On 1 March – Wales's day – a proud nation puts daffodils in its buttonholes as the church remembers its great patron saint, David. He was a sixth-century monk, who founded a monastery in south-west Wales,

believed to have been near where now the tiny
cathedral in the Welsh city of St Davids stands and
is a popular setting for *Songs of Praise*.

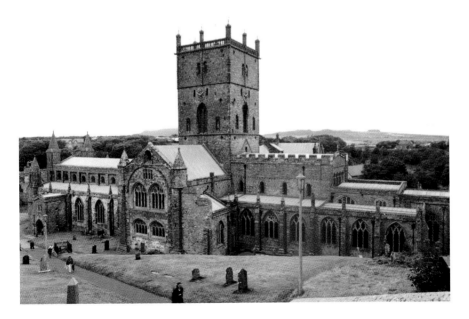

David set demanding standards of prayer and work
for his community, and lived his life simply, not only
without alcohol but also without 'unnecessary
conversation'. Could any Lenten penance be more
challenging? All the same, as anyone will know who
has been on a silent retreat in Lent, while working or
walking out of doors in silence, when the chattering stops, we are
rewarded with an increased awareness of how closely our lives are bound up
with the natural world. Chaffinches calling 'Tsip… cheer… tsip… cheeer!'
seem to keep pace with walkers along the hedgerows of a country lane, flying
from shrub to shrub; in the garden, birds use our hedges and trees to build
their homes, and next month swallows, swifts and martins will arrive from
Africa to build their nests in our garages and sheds; robins use our discarded

garden forks as lookout posts. This Lent, in broad daylight in a town garden, I even saw two immaculately tidy foxes taking the March air together.

If we forgo conversation in Lent, we should not go without singing. The Welsh have taught us the joy of singing, and their passion for music can create 'hwyl' even in the most reticent English congregations. I discovered this in the Hertfordshire town of Berkhamstead, when *Songs of Praise* was being conducted by a short, fiery Welsh clergyman. He had set Baring-Gould's 'Onward Christian Soldiers' to the Welsh tune 'Rachie', and just when the congregation thought they had reached a triumphant end, he wound them up further with the Welsh tradition of repeating the last chorus at least twice. 'With the cross of Jesus going on before!' they bellowed once more, and again once more, and suddenly they all appeared to be hurtling towards the kingdom of heaven led by the wildly exhilarating gestures from the pulpit. I was frantically directing more and more unscripted extra shots from the camera team, until the moment when the conductor's baton flew into pieces in an ecstatic final arc.

The gentle but equally powerful Welsh tune 'Ar hyd y nos' (All through the night) is set in the *Songs of Praise* hymnbook to words which for me reflect the experience of that night in Hertfordshire: 'For the fruits of his creation, thanks be to God.' But when the great Welsh star, Sir Harry Secombe sang an evening hymn in St Saviour's and St Peter's during *Highway*'s visit to Eastbourne, he sang 'Ar hyd y nos' with familiar words written by an Englishman and an Irishman.

God, that madest earth and heaven,
darkness and light;
who the day for toil hast given,
for rest the night;
may thine angel-guards defend us,
slumber sweet thy mercy send us,
holy dreams and hopes attend us,
this livelong night.

Guard us waking, guard us sleeping;
and, when we die,
may we in thy mighty keeping
all peaceful lie:
when the last dread call shall wake us,
do not thou our God forsake us,
but to reign in glory take us
with thee on high.

BISHOP R. HEBER (1783–1826) V. 1
ARCHBISHOP RICHARD WHATELY (1787–1863) V. 2

March Hares

●●●●●●●●●●●●●●

LENT

'March is the month of the hare and the Celtic saint, when it's always Lent, and hardly ever Easter, of lengthening days but icy winds. An appropriate month to commemorate those ancient stoics, David, Patrick and Cuthbert.'

LIZ BARR

This is how Liz began one of her contributions to Radio 4's *Prayer for the Day* a few years ago. Her description of the days of the hare, which I usually only saw in the headlights tearing in all directions in front of my car as I returned home late from work, made me think about the time of thinking and stillness that help make a 'good Lent'. Liz often says that she spends far too much time standing and staring, but as I used to tear around Scotland, chasing the budgets and management schedules of religious broadcasting, her standing and staring became the thinking and stillness that makes good programmes, and not just for Lent. Liz's *Prayer for the Day* about the hares, led into an ancient Celtic prayer:

'... Until recently I lived in a house opposite a field and in March I used to watch those other ancient survivors, the wild mountain hares. All day long they lay motionless, enduring icy gales of hail and snow. Their only warmth, their own body heat reflected back from the little scrape of earth they lay on. Not until the light of day began to fade would they stir. Then one by one they would slowly stretch and move about and eat. Whenever there was a long Midlothian sunset, I would have the pleasure of watching their games begin, the chase, the boxing match, the dance of courtship, before it fell too dark to see. Watching fascinated from my warm cottage, they became for me the model of stoic endurance, with its reward of leaping joy.

'Life for Christians is far more comfortable now than for the ones who walked the path of the old Celtic saints. St Cuthbert's hard road led him from Lindisfarne to Durham and back to die alone in a hermit's cell on the Farne Islands. But we have our own pain. There are many today who might be happier if they could exchange their warm houses, their debts and their doubts for the cold austerity of a cave and the joyful certainty of the love of the brotherhood and the love of God.'

Bless to me, O God,
The earth beneath my foot,
Bless to me, O God,
The path whereon I go;
Bless to me, O God,
The thing of my desire;
Bless to me the thing
Whereon is set my mind,
Bless to me the thing
Whereon is set my love,
Bless to me the thing
Whereon is set my hope;
O Thou King of Kings,
Bless Thou to me mine eye!
CARMINA GADELICA

The Flying Preacher

It was, I soon discovered, quite a tall order to explain *Songs of Praise* to a Finnish TV executive and the director of a Belgian art theatre showing experimental films. We were sitting in a state-of-the-art video-editing suite in Helsinki, and a classic edition of the series, with Sir Harry Secombe presenting, had just been shown. My fellow judges seemed quite baffled by Sir Harry's natural mixture of faith and humour and his tendency to suddenly break into song. Religion, they said, is serious, so how can the 'pastor' be humorous? Luckily, another TV colleague in the room was from Holland, where *Songs of Praise* is well known and from where programmes have sometimes come over the years.

'This is a very British institution,' she said, 'watched religiously every week by millions – we like it too.' Hearing that the programme was so popular and that Sir Harry was one of Britain's best-loved comedians seemed only to baffle them further. It was obvious that I was failing to get *Songs of Praise* included in the finalists for the world's top religious TV awards.

A week spent viewing religious TV with other Europeans made me realize that although language and culture create their own barriers, the Christian gospel ignores all frontiers. We judges became good friends as we tried to agree on the best of 118 different programmes made in many languages and ranging from Finland to Tibet, via St Paul's Cathedral. On arrival in Helsinki, our Finnish hosts had greeted us and given us a meticulously prepared schedule that announced that we would be watching 66 hours of TV in just a week. We all wondered what we had let ourselves in for, and knowing that after little more than half an hour of viewing at home I usually fall into dreamless slumber, I asked that we view in a room with all the lights on.

Fortunately, after the first session, the next day was Sunday and we all agreed on a late start. While my colleagues slept in, I felt the need to be in touch with the familiar surroundings of the Anglican Church, so I set out on a journey through Helsinki which became like a scene from a John Le Carré novel with a dash of *Dr Zhivago* thrown in.

I could have simply settled for the Lutheran cathedral in the centre of the city, or the famous Temppeliaukio Church hollowed out of solid rock. Instead I chose the Mikael Agricola Church, which our friends at Finnish TV only knew as a place to which other visitors sometimes set off, to attend a church service in English – but nobody remembered their returning to tell the tale.

Although our Finnish TV hosts spoke in English, which was their third language, to make me welcome, I was armed with a guidebook as I waited in the snow at a deserted tram stop. I could read 'Missä on Mikael Agricola Kirko?' (Where is the Mikael Agricola Church?), but could I say it, let alone understand the answer?

The tram driver allowed me to get halfway through my first Finnish phrase before, without even glancing at me, he gave me a ticket which, he told me in perfect English, meant that I could spend a day riding trams – my personal idea of heaven.

I was the only passenger as we rumbled down into the city through deserted streets. It did not look as if many Finns were churchgoers. Eventually the driver gestured that I should get off, pointing to another tram apparently going in the other direction. It must have been waiting for me, for again I was the only passenger as we squealed our way around so many right-angled turns that I lost all sense of direction. We passed a harbour with boats tightly imprisoned by the ice and then began to accelerate up through yet more deserted streets.

In a vague panic, and fearing I had somehow got involved in some weird Le Carré plot, I rang the bell and got off. The tram shot off into the distance and I began to slither alone along the icy pavement. By pure chance, I eventually came to a huge brown building inscribed 'Mikael Agricola'.

All its doors were closed. In fact it did not look as if they had been opened for years, but there was a small notice to read – in Finnish.

As I got the phrase book out again, a short, bearded man, almost the first human being who wasn't a tram driver that I had seen since I left the hotel, suddenly appeared around the corner. His fur hat was clearly a practical defence against the bitingly cold wind rather than a disguise, but I was startled when he said – in English – 'You have come for the service, but today the church is closed while they make a TV recording.'

The travel-stained *Songs of Praise* producer had had his one morning off TV viewing thwarted by TV, but I was only briefly disappointed. 'But we will gather the other stragglers,' said the man, 'and then I will drive you all to a service.'

I can think of no similar circumstances in Britain where such a generous gesture would be made, where a member of a congregation would wait around in the freezing cold on the off chance strangers might turn up for a service and be disappointed. It could have been that nobody had come, but as we stood in the winter sunshine, stamping the snow off our feet, two more people appeared.

There was just enough room for us all to cram into our guide's tiny car and hurtle through the streets, which were now coming to life. We whistled past the golden domes of Europe's largest Orthodox cathedral and up a bewildering number of narrow streets, including travelling the wrong way up at least one one-way street. And it still felt a bit like the beginning of a Le Carré spy mystery by the time we were climbing the stairs of an office block. That too, of course, was deserted.

Climbing the stairwell in these odd surroundings, I heard the growing sound of a congregation singing 'All my hope on God is founded'. I suddenly felt at home.

Our guide introduced us to one of the friendliest congregations I have ever met. Like the 118 programmes that I was to watch that week, they seemed to have come from every part of the world. Exiled in a real 'upper room' were Christians for whom home in Helsinki is the St Nicholas Chaplaincy, and who meet wherever they can find a room.

After the service, and brimming with energy, I was ready to walk through the streets to visit the Lutheran cathedral, which everyone said I must see. Well it was there, somewhere, behind a quite colossal amount of broadcasting equipment, including mammoth cranes from which were suspended enough TV lights to illuminate St Paul's Cathedral. I realized that it was time to give in and get down to viewing television programmes.

After my strange pilgrimage, it is a German programme called *The Flying Preacher* that I most recall from the next four days of watching TV 12 hours a day. I was ashamed to admit to my fellow jury members from Belgium and Holland that this terrific story from England was one about which I knew nothing.

Accompanied by a solemn German commentary, the film showed what must be one of the most eccentric acts of evangelism of all time. The first scene was of Stonehenge, our mysterious pagan monument on Salisbury Plain. What proceedings were underway there I cannot now recall, as they were soon

interrupted by the wasp-like buzzing of a tiny microlight aircraft. It looked like a sort of aerial deckchair attached to a mower engine, and as it circled slowly over the monument, the pilot produced a loud hailer and, directing it at the ground, broke into a chorus of the hymn 'How great thou art'.

It was a risky but utterly original way of proclaiming the gospel in a material world where everyone else makes use of stunts to attract attention. Because the programme made me laugh, it also made me think, and in the scenes that followed, German viewers were able to see the good effect of the work of an eccentric Pentecostal pastor in one of the toughest housing estates of England.

'Why should the devil have all the best stunts?' I said when asked for my verdict. My colleagues were unimpressed. 'Too many laughs,' they said, crossing out the entry.

All the same, like the gesture of my bearded friend outside the Mikael Agricola Church, this was someone really 'going out into the hedgerows and the highways'. Without seeing it, I for one would have been the poorer.

St Patrick's Day

●●●●●●●●●●●●●●

17 MARCH

Almighty God,
Who in your providence chose your servant Patrick
to be the apostle of the Irish people:
keep alive in us the fire of the faith he kindled
and strengthen us in our pilgrimage
towards the light of everlasting life;
through Jesus Christ your Son our Lord,
who is alive and reigns with you,
in the unity of the Holy Spirit,
one God, now and forever.

COMMON WORSHIP: SERVICES AND PRAYERS FOR THE CHURCH OF ENGLAND

SPRING:
APRIL TO MAY

Tell Me a Story

● ● ● ● ● ● ● ● ● ● ● ● ● ●

APRIL
Father, hearing children scream,
Threw them in a nearby stream,
Saying as he drowned the third,
Children should be seen, not heard.

ANON

That appalling little rhyme was chosen for me to recite as my contribution to the entertainment at a children's party when I was ten years old. I was a silent child, who tried hard to avoid any such organized events, having been resentful of fellow guests ever since I had first learnt the hard way that there were other children than me in the world. It is almost my earliest memory, sitting aged three on the rag rug in our tiny cottage in wartime Wiltshire and discovering a brightly wrapped package. I was just opening it when a hand snatched it away and a stern voice gave me the first rebuke of my life: 'That's not for you! There are other children in the world, you know.'

I *didn't* know. Not until then.

It took a long time to get over the shock, and the baleful rhyme would have suited my mood at a party, as well as been short enough for me to stand knock-kneed in front of the assembled company and recite by heart. It must have been a rare success, for a photograph was taken of the grinning recitalist and his audience.

Nearly half a century later, Liz and I have often lain awake through what feels like most of the night, hearing from the spare bedroom the cries and squeaks of one of our three grandchildren, heralding them all waking up and joining in. The nasty little rhyme would come briefly back into my head, and then I would remind myself of my other 'thought for the day' (or rather the night) about children: 'One of these little children may one day be prime minister or archbishop of Canterbury'.

I must have got that idea from my own grandiose dreams of what I would be when I grew up. Yet even as I write this, it is quite possible that a future ruler, pope or archbishop of Canterbury is preparing to take their first breath… or drawing in a deep breath prior to screaming for their mother in the middle of the night. These sleep-dislocating cries in the small hours are a reminder of the vulnerable dependency of the very young child and I do *try* to think of them as a gift from God. For whatever mess our generation makes of the world, the small squeakers will one day have to deal with at least some of it. Even the philosopher, Bryan Magee, without any religious affiliations, movingly describes a newborn child like this: 'A light comes on in a new centre of consciousness, and it is another one of us… We inherit a going concern.'

When they were small, our own trio would often all be in full cry by 4 a.m. While 'Granny' Liz and I feigned sleep, their mother would eventually wake from her own deep slumber. We would hear her low voice and their high-pitched protests about something or other, but she would soon settle them down again, without us moving. She always enjoys staying in our home – knowing that we are there to help and share her exhausting world for a few days… And for nearly 15 years now we have watched as her three squealing babies have one by one, and with a lot more charm than I ever had, morphed into young human beings I can reason with.

Songs of Praise viewers, too, have been watching a boy grow up, from soaring treble to sensitive tenor. In the mid-1980s an angelic choirboy from Bangor first appeared as *Songs of Praise*'s youngest presenter ever, and many viewers, I suspect, see themselves as Aled Jones's honorary 'TV' grandparents. I do know, because I was one of them, that the producers of ITV's rival programme, *Highway*, were trembling in their boots when Aled arrived on *Songs of Praise*, even though what we had to offer was also a wonderful singer and the kindest 'grandad' in the world, Harry Secombe. A few years later BBC audience researchers were to report that Harry 'made life complete' for many viewers when he, too, joined the *Songs of Praise* family.

Once I ducked a bedtime request to read yet again a familiar story by inventing a ridiculous one of my own. I was hoping to wear out the boys' energy and make them sleepy by foxing them with characters with similar names: Morris, Boris and Doris. I borrowed Ernest, the policeman, from 'Toy Town' of distant *Children's Hour* memory, and added a policewoman called Tracey, and a baddy called Nurse Handy, drawn from childhood memories of a distant family friend, who in certain moods would rush around our house brandishing a hairbrush, much to my brother's and my great delight.

After five episodes on successive nights, James, Max and Charlie were far from sleepy when my own invention finally ran out. Sitting three in a row on the spare-room bed, they would watch me closely, waiting for the opportunity to pounce every time I made a slip. The details of my story had become far more complex than I could cope with, but they were always quite clear about the intricacies of earlier episodes, and they soon realized that I had completely confused myself with Morris, Boris and Doris. I was on the run – and they pursued me for some years about the outcome of my ludicrous plot.

So, with no sign of a yawn, they would go over to Granny Liz, who had stolen and adapted the plot from Philip Pullman's *Northern Lights* to build a violent and bloodthirsty suspense story of three boys who flew up from Devon to Scotland on dragon's wings to help angels and witches battle giant armoured bears and rescue stolen children from their snowbound prison in the north. Soon toy daggers slipped to the floor, and they were all peacefully asleep, safe in the belief that their grandmother was the greatest storyteller in the world. It was to be a few years before her deception was found out, when they read the originals for themselves.

If I had known as a child what I have learned from watching our grandchildren growing up, my own childhood might have been a far happier experience. My brother and I lived almost entirely separate lives from the adult members of our family, but our grandchildren treat Liz and me like each other, and only slightly inferior. Questions about God are lobbed without warning into adult conversations. 'Is God dead?' asked the youngest grandchild, aged five, from the back of the car at a particularly hazardous road junction. Before I could answer, the other two had dealt with the question and conducted a conversation about Jesus rising from the dead and other theological matters that I had scarcely begun to think about until I was 21. As I approached the railway station in Edinburgh, fretting about parking, the middle grandson looked up at the big crucifix on Old St Paul's Church. 'Why is that man hanging on the wall?' he said.

'Don't be stupid,' said the youngest, 'that's Jesus.'

But now, with their mother and father, James, Max and Charlie will soon be starting a new life on the far side of the world. On the North Island of New Zealand, overlooking a beautiful bay in the southern ocean, they are going to build their own home, where they will grow from children into young men. As we reluctantly let them go, we know it is important not to think of them only in the light of often-repeated stories of their childhood, especially not by our own tales of middle-of-the-night squeaks,
which are already received with bored disdain by the eldest. And I won't bother any more to remember my nasty little childhood rhyme. At the same time, I believe, childhood should not be altogether forgotten. It is not all of who we are, but it will always be part of who we become.

MY COUSINS CODY AND HAYLEY

In fact, other generations of my family are also living in the southern hemisphere, with my young cousin's three children growing up in Australia. Easter in the southern hemisphere comes as the leaves fall off the trees and the days grow darker. It may make the events of the first Easter seem all the more astonishing and all the more wonderful. And in the end, will it matter which hemisphere we find ourselves in? All these emerging young minds are turning Christmas into Easter for us all.

If you think in years – plant flowers;
If you think in decades – plant trees;
If you think in centuries – educate children.
CHINESE PROVERB

Can Do

● ● ● ● ● ● ● ● ● ● ● ● ● ● ●

PALM SUNDAY

They were approaching Jerusalem, and when they reached Bethphage at the mount of Olives Jesus sent off two disciples, and told them: 'Go into the village opposite, where you will at once find a donkey tethered with her foal beside her. Untie them, and bring them to me. If anyone says anything to you, answer, "The Master needs them"; and he will let you have them at once.'

This was to fulfil the prophecy which says, 'Tell the daughter of Zion, "Here is your king, who comes to you in gentleness, riding on a donkey, on the foal of a beast of burden".'

The disciples went and did as Jesus had directed, and brought the donkey and her foal; they laid their cloaks on them and Jesus mounted. Crowds of people carpeted the road with their cloaks, and some cut branches from the trees to spread in his path. Then the crowds in front and behind raised the shout: 'Hosanna to the Son of David! Blessed is he who comes in the name of the Lord! Hosanna in the heavens!'

When he entered Jerusalem the whole city went wild with excitement. 'Who is this?' people asked, and the crowds replied, 'This is the prophet Jesus, from Nazareth in Galilee.'

MATTHEW 21:1–11

Liz and I worked together in the 1980s to make a video as part of the Church of England's 'Faith in the City' initiative. We called it *Can Do* and featured only stories of people who were struggling to survive in the inner cities. We did not include professional church or social workers, only the people who were themselves at the sharp end, the poor and disadvantaged who had the faith and determination to keep going. We hoped that our video about these usually unsung heroes, whose own efforts were helping rejuvenate their communities, would be a great fund-raiser to help other less successful people caught in the poverty trap.

Audiences around the country were impressed and moved, but mainly declined to dig into their pockets for people who were so evidently making such a great success of life. We learned the annoying lesson that it is victims, not people who refuse to be victims, who attract the most support.

There were no victims among the congregation at the parish church of St Mary of Eton in Hackney Wick on Palm Sunday. The film crew had to run through the nearby housing estate to keep up with them as they paraded between the tower blocks singing Palm Sunday hymns, and if nobody laid

HACKNEY STATION, AND WATERCRESS PLANTATION.

their cloaks for them, they at least attracted a lot of faces to the windows of the tower blocks.

Before we began filming, their priest, Father Duncan Ross, who was at one time adviser and model for the 'vicar' in *EastEnders*, had told us about his own arrival at St Mary of Eton. He was brought up in India, and after spending some time as a curate at another parish, St Mary of Eton was to be his 'own' first parish. He arrived full of plans and excitement, only to find the church buildings dilapidated, damp and empty, and the church finances long neglected and deeply in the red. Instead of being able to minister to the people of the parish, he found he was spending all his time in meetings with bankers and builders. One day, after coping with floods and collapsing gutters, and feeling more and more of a failure, he returned to the vicarage in the pouring rain with his two shopping bags, and had just reached the front door when both bags burst and all his shopping rolled around in the mud. He looked up, and over the vicarage door, he suddenly saw illuminated words in big letters: 'It is impossible.'

Oh! he thought. I see. It is impossible. It was a message from the angels. He knew then that everything was all right. He wasn't a failure. It was impossible, so he just had to do his best. He went on to build up one of the liveliest, most energized congregations either of us had ever come across.

All glory, laud and honour
to thee, Redeemer, King,
to whom the lips of children
made sweet hosannas ring.

Thou art the King of Israel,
thou David's royal Son,
who in the Lord's name comest,
the King and blessèd One.

The company of angels
are praising thee on high,
and mortal men and all things
created make reply.

The people of the Hebrews
with palms before thee went;
our praise and prayer and anthems
before thee we present.

To thee before thy passion
they sang their hymns of praise;
to thee now high exalted
our melody we raise.

ST THEODULPH OF ORLEANS, (C. 760–821)
TR. J.M. NEALE (1818–66) ALTD

The President's Bible Class

●●●●●●●●●●●●●●

After singing the Passover hymn, they went out to the mount of Olives. And Jesus said to them, 'You will all lose faith; for it is written: "I will strike the shepherd and the sheep will be scattered." Nevertheless, after I am raised I shall go ahead of you into Galilee.'

Peter answered, 'Everyone else may lose faith, but I will not.'

Jesus said to him, 'Truly I tell you: today, this very night, before the cock crows twice, you yourself will disown me three times.'

But Peter insisted: 'Even if I have to die with you, I will never disown you.' And they all said the same.

MARK 14:26–31

It was just another Sunday at First Baptist Church in Washington D.C. Together with film maker and *Songs of Praise* producer, Norman Stone, I had been invited to go along, and we were advised to arrive in time for the Bible class before the service. As I hadn't been to a Bible class since my childhood days, when coloured stamps of Bible scenes – the reward for being the 'least disruptive pupil' – were all that I took away with me, it seemed a good idea to catch up.

We were shown into a small, simple room, where a few adults were already studying Bibles and reading the story of Peter denying Jesus after his arrest in the garden of Gethsemane. I'm sure everyone always recognizes themselves in Peter in this story, and I knew from past experience that it would probably encourage me to make even more fervent promises than Peter's, and then realize I had broken them long before the dawn cockcrow. I began to wonder how I might leave the room without being overcome by shame.

The atmosphere changed dramatically with the sudden arrival of a number of stockily built, shiny-suited men who, rather than sitting down, took up positions around the wall with folded arms. They did not smile at us and the tension began to resemble that in the high priest Caiaphas's courtyard, where Peter had followed Jesus.

One of the high priest's servant-girls came by and saw him there warming himself. She looked closely at him and said, 'You were with this man from Nazareth, this Jesus.'

But he denied it: 'I know nothing', he said; 'I have no idea what you are talking about,' and he went out into the forecourt. The servant-girl saw him there and began

to say again to the bystanders, 'He is one of them;' and again he denied it.
MARK 14:66–70

Until this day in 1980, the nearest I had ever been to the American Secret
Service was watching the film *All the President's Men* about the Watergate
break-in and the unseating of President Nixon. The men who had joined us
for the Bible class were all wearing earpieces – and clearly not so that they
could listen to a sports commentary, as one elderly member of our Matins
congregation in Kent disgracefully used to do during the vicar's sermon when
Sunday cricket first began. Our stern-faced companions lining the wall tensed
up even more when, without any fanfares, the president of the United States
came in and quietly sat down. Our Bible class teacher had arrived.

James Earl Carter, the 39th President, a Democrat, was in the run-up
to the presidential election and facing a very tough challenge from the
Hollywood star and Republican, Ronald Reagan. In our small room in
Washington, we were beginning our study of Peter's experience with a global
peacemaker, who had just brought about the Middle East Peace Agreement
between Prime Minister Begin from Israel and Egypt's President Sadat.

President Carter tried whenever he could to fit this Bible study at his church
into his impossible schedule. From the moment he sat down and asked for
a volunteer to read Mark's story again to us, it was clear that he was a born
teacher. Since we couldn't expect the Secret Service to say much, it was
obviously going to be down to our small group to contribute to the
discussion that followed. The president was inclined not to throw questions
into the ring, but to turn and look directly at one of us. Some of the group
were evidently relaxed with a friend with whom they regularly studied the
Bible, but for Norman and me it seemed astonishing that he listened so
intently to the various answers we offered, as the terrible human dilemma
for Peter on the last night of Jesus' life was teased out.

Again, a little later, the bystanders said to Peter, 'You must be one of them; you are a
Galilean.' At this he started to curse, and declared with an oath, 'I do not know this
man you are talking about.'

At that moment the cock crowed for the second time; and Peter remembered how Jesus had said to him, 'Before the cock crows twice, you will disown me three times.' And he burst into tears.
MARK 14:70–72

'You know,' said the president of the United States looking around at the small group, 'that guy Peter's experience is really saying something to me.' For a moment, Jimmy Carter seemed suddenly troubled and weary, as though while he had been travelling the length and breadth of the U.S.A. in the run-up to the election, he had become more and more aware that the faces of America's poor were never far behind the crowds and celebrities and fellow politicians cheering him on. Whatever plans had succeeded or failed, it appeared to me that he felt that he had not lived up to his own expectations of himself, nor to the faith that brought him to church. That anyway was the thought that hung in the air as the session ended. He stood and shook hands with all of us, friends and strangers, and then was gone. The room seemed very empty without the Secret Servicemen.

A few months later, Jimmy Carter was decisively beaten by Ronald Reagan, rejected by the constituency that perhaps he felt that he had let down and the promises that he felt he had betrayed.

Ten years on, I had another encounter with Jimmy Carter, as we filmed his project to build affordable houses for poor people. It was a scheme depending on very fast work to keep the costs down and ex-President Carter was filmed hands-on, carrying and fixing roof timbers himself. Cynics might have thought it was all just a show for the cameras, but our extraordinary Sunday morning's Bible study in the small room in Washington, where not a moment was filmed, recorded or reported, convinces me otherwise.

I have been thinking a lot about that darkest night in the gospel, and Peter's broken promises, during the publicity campaign for Mel Gibson's film about the last 12 hours in the life of Jesus. No amount of on-screen violence can so tellingly bring home to us the part we all play in the suffering and death of Christ as much as that human story of betrayal in the courtyard, before the cock crowed twice. But, unlike the terrified disciples that night, we know that in two days it will be Easter, and that God's response to all our betrayals is forgiveness – for them, for Jimmy Carter, for me and for you.

O sacred head, sore wounded,
with grief and pain weighed down,
how scornfully surrounded
with thorns, thine only crown!
How pale art thou with anguish,
with sore abuse and scorn!
How does that visage languish,
which once was bright as morn!

What language shall I borrow
to praise thee, dearest friend,
for this thy dying sorrow,
thy pity without end?
Lord, make me thine for ever,
nor let me faithless prove;
O let me never, never
abuse such dying love!

Be near me when I'm dying,
O show thy cross to me,
that I, for succour flying,
my eyes may fix on thee;
these eyes, new faith receiving,
from Jesus shall not move;
for whoso dies believing,
dies safely through thy love.

ATTRIB. BERNARD OF CLAIRVAUX (1091–1153)
TR. PAUL GERHARDT (1607–76)
TR. J.W. ALEXANDER (1804–59), ALTD

Easter People: Joan and Colin

● ● ● ● ● ● ● ● ● ● ● ● ● ●

EASTER DAY

When the sabbath was over, Mary of Magdala, Mary the mother of James, and Salome brought aromatic oils, intending to go and anoint him; and very early on the first day of the week, just after sunrise, they came to the tomb.

They were wondering among themselves who would roll

away the stone for them from the entrance to the tomb, when they looked up and saw that the stone, huge as it was, had been rolled back already. They went into the tomb, where they saw a young man sitting on the right-hand side, wearing a white robe; and they were dumbfounded. But he said to them, 'Do not be alarmed; you are looking for Jesus of Nazareth, who was crucified. He has been raised; he is not here. Look, there is the place where they laid him. But go and say to his disciples and to Peter: "He is going ahead of you into Galilee; there you will see him, as he told you."'

Then they went out and ran away from the tomb, trembling with amazement. They said nothing to anyone, for they were afraid.

And they delivered all these instructions briefly to Peter and his companions. Afterwards Jesus himself sent out by them, from east to west, the sacred and imperishable message of eternal salvation.

MARK 16:1–8

When Joan first invited young Colin round to her home for tea, he was very frightened. It should have been the other way round, for the last time Colin had met Joan, he had been holding a knife to her throat.

Joan and Colin's story was told in the year 2004, on the Easter Sunday *Songs of Praise* from Johannesburg. This Easter Festival programme was to mark the tenth anniversary of the first free elections in South Africa since the days of apartheid.

'Ten years ago something close to a miracle happened here,' said the presenter, Jonathan Edwards, in his introduction, explaining that as the country publicly celebrated a decade of democracy, he was there to meet some of the unsung heroes who are continually working behind the scenes

to help South Africa reflect the new life of an Easter nation.

One Sunday in 1990 'live' TV pictures, watched all over the world, showed us one of the most momentous events of our time. For what seemed ages, the cameras showed a long, straight road, and in the foreground we glimpsed now and again a surging gaggle of news reporters desperate to be the first to speak to the man who was expected at any moment to appear out of the dusty landscape. The whole world was waiting to see Nelson Mandela emerging down that long, empty road, after 27 years in jail, where he had been imprisoned with robbers and murderers for his political opposition to the apartheid regime.

After what had seemed an endless wait, the cameras picked out a group of figures in the far distance, and then a man unseen for so many years, greyer but easily recognizable, approached with a dignified, firm step. It is impossible to imagine what he was thinking, but the ex-convict already had the bearing of the head of state that he was to become as President Mandela. It was an Easter moment not only for South Africans, but for every one of us.

It was only later that we learned that the warm but rather restrained smile with which he responded to the rapturous welcome he received from the crowds was partly because, in his humanity, and in the confusion of leaving the detention camp on Robin Island for ever, he had also left behind his glasses and the text of the speech he had prepared.

In spite of all the euphoria and our hopes on that day, life in South Africa, liberated from race laws in a new democratic era achieved with an almost miraculous lack of violence, largely through the greatness and grace of its first president, is still difficult. Its people have to contend with the economic and health problems that have beset the whole continent. Up to a million people in South Africa today are either infected with HIV or have Aids; orphaned children live and run wild on the streets and, as in so many other parts of the world, increasing numbers of people, black and white, are becoming the victims of drug-related violent crime. This was how Colin and Joan's lives first came together.

Joan is in her early 70s and from an Afrikaans background. She and her husband and son live in Johannesburg in a poor district where crime is commonplace. One wet Monday morning, she was at home alone, working at her computer. Suddenly two black men appeared in her room. They had stealthily removed the glass from her window and one of them began ransacking the house while the other tied Joan up. Then, pressing a knife at the back of her neck, they robbed her of all her few treasures, even forcing her to give up her wedding ring.

Although the police were called, it was a black neighbour, Israel, who caught the robbers nearby and locked them in his own van. When the police came to arrest them, Joan was able to look again at her attackers.

'One of them begged me to save him,' Joan told Jonathan Edwards, 'but I gave him a look that said, "Go to hell and kill yourself." He had chosen me, a pensioner, because I would be too weak to fight back. He could go to prison and die there; I couldn't even consider the possibility of him bettering himself.'

He did go to prison, sentenced to seven years, and Joan tried to put him out of her mind.

Colin, the boy with the knife, was then a teenager. He had grown up in a home where all problems were dealt with by aggressive and violent behaviour. His mother and father, both alcoholics, had eventually separated and his father found a new partner, who told Colin his mother had left him because of his bad behaviour. Colin made friends on the streets with boys who found their confidence in crime and drugs. He said, 'I admired them, 'cos they had direction and no one could stop them. They were heroes.'

Colin's own crimes grew more violent. He held up a security guard with a toy gun and stole a real gun from him. One of his friends, whom he had introduced to crime, was killed in a carjacking that went wrong, but even though he felt guilty, Colin found it impossible to change his ways. 'It had become my only way of life; the only thing that gave me hope. Other criminals gave me the respect I needed.'

Colin still remembers the moment he was arrested after the attempted robbery of Joan. 'I was full of anger. I had been caught by a black guy. How could he do this to me? When Joan looked at me, it was complete hatred.'

While in prison, Colin was introduced to Khulisa, a programme that tries to rehabilitate offenders. He first noticed that working with HIV prisoners, Khulisa offered a new way of life.

'I thought if these guys can change, let me see where I can go.'

The Khulisa programme sounds simple, helping individuals to see themselves as others see them. It was far from simple for Colin. First, in prison he was disowned by other inmates for wanting to change his ways, and then, when he was released, his family and former friends refused to believe that he had changed. They thought it wouldn't last.

Colin felt bad about his crimes, and particularly bad about Joan. One morning, the Khulisa team arranged for Colin to visit Joan at home, to apologize to her. When they got there, he lost his nerve and deliberately led the team to the wrong house.

'Apologizing was the right thing to do, I knew, but approaching her street it all came back to me. I could not do it.'

Joan had been very suspicious when someone had first appeared at her door and said that Colin wanted to ask her to forgive him. 'She told me that Colin could not move on with his life until he had done this.' Joan still felt angry, 'But I also thought, who am I to not accept his apology and roll a stone in front of this young man trying to better his life?'

But Colin did not come to her home that day, and it was only after Colin agreed to return to the prison and make his apology to Joan in front of other inmates that the two met.

On *Songs of Praise*, Joan took up the story, 'I saw this nice young man, who'd grown a couple of inches. Gone was that horrible thing that had held a knife at my throat. I couldn't think of the little wretch any more and I already felt quite proud of him. Then Colin said, "I'm very, very sorry. I want you to forgive me."'

'Of course, Colin,' I said, 'and we had our arms around each other.'

Colin had been shaking with fear as he walked forward. He told Jonathan, 'I kept thinking, what would I feel if someone threatened to cut off my fingers? Joan gave me a hug and her lipstick got on my shirt and to this day, I've never washed it.'

Colin remembered how Joan's eyes, too, were different. 'In her eyes I saw hope, I saw everything. It's like I was being born again. Whenever there's a problem, I always think back to that day.'

So Joan invited Colin to tea. Colin admitted that he took a friend along for support. 'I didn't expect her to be so friendly. I thought she would be frightened too. Now I am welcome there any time.'

What Colin did not know is that Joan was the only person who was willing to forgive. Others, having been through the Khulisa programme, and wanting to make amends, have been turned down. Even Joan's friends said that she was stupid to forgive.

Joan says that as a Christian, 'Forgiveness is not an option, it's a must.'

This, however, is not a story with a tidy, totally happy ending. Colin's life in Soweto has continued to be very hard. He has to fight every day against his old addiction to crime, and seeing people who he once wronged shakes his confidence in himself. Seeing their reaction makes him, too, wonder whether he really has made a clean break with the past. 'I have to take it a day at a time.'

For Joan, life has taken a further cruel turn. She has again been attacked at home, and this time her only son was killed and her husband left disabled and hardly able to speak. For now, she cannot find the way to forgive these killers. 'Colin took things, but the other people took my son. How can I forgive that?'

Perhaps the words of a fellow Christian, Colin Morris, could help both Joan and young Colin. 'God is morally consistent, he does not play games. But he never shows anybody a way out of a predicament, only through it.'

Dr Colin Morris, former president of the Methodist Conference and a distinguished broadcaster and preacher, served as a missionary in Northern Rhodesia for several years during the time when it was being reborn as the Republic of Zambia led by Kenneth Kaunda. Both Colin Morris and Kenneth Kaunda had been detained during the campaign to gain Zambia's independence. Colin remembers visiting the then unknown Kenneth Kaunda in jail: 'The Northern Rhodesian administration had just said that it would be a thousand years before the country was handed over to the African people. I found Kaunda sitting on the floor of the jail, drawing up his future cabinet.'

COLIN MORRIS

Seven years later, Kaunda was president.

'Man knows God is around because things are changing,' Colin preached in a sermon in St James's Piccadilly. This made a big impact on me when it was broadcast in the 1980s.

'A people with a destiny must be kept on the move. With Jesus, things began to move again, and new power came to an old religion. So they took him and nailed him down – but the God who will have change, smashed the tomb.'

Archbishop Desmond Tutu, who in the land of his birth had the vote for the first time at the age of 62, said on *Songs of Praise,* 'Could anything have been more hopeless than a young man strung up on a cross on a Friday and darkness enveloping the world? And then Easter happens.'

Lord of the Dance

● ● ● ● ● ● ● ● ● ● ● ● ● ●

EASTERTIDE

Sydney Carter, who died in March 2004, wrote songs that cannot be pigeonholed. For a long time they were heard rather than printed, being performed by the folksinger/songwriter in pubs, prisons and, at least once, in the middle of an ice rink during the Edinburgh Festival. Then one day he was invited into a church, to perform *Lord of the Dance*, his great song of resurrection, although even then, only below ground, down in the crypt. This experience perhaps inspired the line in his satirical song, *The Vicar is a Beatnik*, about a shocked congregation reacting to their trendy vicar: 'We're digging out the crypt to make a discotheque.'

As always with Sydney, the finger points both ways, for another line in the same song goes: 'We love the Church of England – although we never go.'

Sydney Carter's range of styles and songs included *One Last Cigarette* in which the late Sheila Hancock perfected the musical 'smoker's cough', and *Down Below*, a funny if slightly sinister tale of life below the city streets, made popular by Ian Wallace.

Sydney Carter was at his best with Christian songs that demanded an active response, songs like *When I Needed a Neighbour* and *I Come Like a Beggar*. Having served in wartime with the Friends' Ambulance Unit in the Middle East and Greece, Sydney Carter found great spiritual strength in the Quaker movement, although he also always felt the necessity to 'Travel on, travel on'.

Bell and book and candle
Cannot hold him any more,
For the bird is flying
As he did before.

Ah! The bird of heaven!
Follow where the bird has gone;
If you want to find him,
Keep on travelling on.
FROM *BIRD OF HEAVEN*, SYDNEY CARTER (1915–2004)

Lord of the Dance, perhaps his finest work, is a hymn for all seasons, but is above all as direct and powerful an account of the suffering, death and resurrection of Jesus as any hymn we sing each Easter.

I was used to hearing it sung rather ponderously, but in the summer of 1976, John Bertalot, then master of music at Blackburn Cathedral, transformed a huge congregation into a dancing choir as they sang it for the first *Songs of Praise* to be transmitted with filmed interviews of local people choosing their favourite hymns. Had he been present, Sydney Carter, one of the great revolutionary songwriters of the twentieth century, would have called a kindly 'bravo' – but perhaps only given it five out of ten. And had he then been invited to take over as soloist, the tempo of the singing would have doubled, the organ been replaced by a kazoo or a small drum, and the words sung in the present tense, which was how he preferred to sing it.

Sydney claimed that you could tell if a hymn was any good if it could survive being sung in a folk club, or in any other unlikely place.

'Scriptures and creeds may come to seem incredible,' he wrote, 'but faith will still go dancing on.'

Lord of the Dance grew out of the author's interest in the Shaker sect of North America, which had its beginning in eighteenth-century Manchester. The Shakers use dance to express their spiritual life, and it is one of their own hymns, 'Simple Gifts', that is the source of the now well-known tune to *Lord of the Dance*.

Once, when filming Sydney Carter, I watched as he taught a village primary school to 'do' *Lord of the Dance*. They were fascinated by what must have seemed to them like a very old man with a small drum. He could hardly contain himself from dancing.

I danced in the morning when the world was begun,
And I danced in the moon and the stars and the sun,
I came down from heaven and I danced on the earth;
At Bethlehem I had my birth.

> *Dance, then, wherever you may be;*
> *I am the Lord of the Dance, said he,*
> *And I'll lead you all, wherever you may be,*
> *And I'll lead you all in the dance, said he.*

SYDNEY CARTER

I danced for the scribe and the Pharisee,
But they would not dance and they would not
   follow me.
I danced for the fishermen, for James and John –
They came with me and the dance went on.

I danced on the Sabbath and I cured the lame;
The holy people said it was a shame.
They whipped and they stripped and they hung me
   on high;
And they left me there on a Cross to die.

I danced on a Friday when the sky turned black –
It's hard to dance with the devil on your back.
They buried my body and they thought I'd gone;
But I am the Dance and I still go on.

They cut me down and I leapt up high;
I am the life that will never, never die;
I'll live in you if you'll live in me –
I am the Lord of the Dance, said he.

The Green Blade Riseth

● ● ● ● ● ● ● ● ● ● ● ● ● ●

EASTERTIDE

'Awake, O north wind, and come, O south wind!
Blow upon my garden, let its fragrance be wafted abroad.'

WORDS OF BLESSING SPOKEN BY THE ARCHBISHOP OF CANTERBURY, ROWAN
WILLIAMS, AT THE ENTRANCE TO THE GARDEN OF THE NEW LONDON
HEADQUARTERS OF THE WORLDWIDE ANGLICAN CHURCH

Once it must have been a traditional cottage garden, packed with herbs, vegetables, foxgloves and sweet williams, for at the end of the new, forty-foot long concrete path was a traditional cottage – my new home. But in the spring of 1981, after serving as a dump while village builders gave the old house a makeover and installed indoor plumbing, all that was left in the garden were an old apple tree, some briar roses and a rich crop of couch grass.

Still, I thought that this little plot would be just about manageable, compared with the large suburban garden I had recently left, which was heaving with fast-track weeds and plantains and moss masquerading as grass. This small, sloping, rectangular patch I had just acquired seemed to me like the garden of Eden, not so much because of what I could see in it, but because of what I could see from it. Over the straggling, long unattended hedge was a greater garden, a view across the orchards of the best part of the Garden of England, the Weald of Kent, stretching from Charing in the East to Linton in the West.

I was making a new start, back in the county of my childhood, and had arrived in time to watch the Wealden spring spread across to the North Downs; and, of course, to conjure some new life out of my little patch of couch grass.

The house had been built in the late fifteenth century as a small, aisled 'hall house', probably the home of quite a rich yeoman. Apart from some small side rooms, including a 'solar', where you might have found privacy, the household lived around an open fire in the middle of the great central hall. The first chimney in the house was not built until the house was already 100 years old, so it must have been a smoky existence. After its early glory days, the hall house had been divided and subdivided many times over the centuries. Complete with Elizabethan bricks, the huge fireplace was now in 'my' part of the divided building, and the first mark I made on the garden was to build a big stack of logs, after the local woodman had stopped his lorry outside the wicket gate and hurled mini tree trunks all over the couch grass. Some fell so heavily that in getting them up I could see that a promisingly rich-looking topsoil lay beneath the grass.

I also set up a birdbath, chiselled in 1976 from Purbeck stone by a stonemason I had filmed choosing a hymn for *Songs of Praise* from Swanage. For nearly 30 years, the birds of Kent, and nowadays Scotland, have bathed in it.

Exploring my small cottage with its disproportionately vast Elizabethan inglenook, I realized that some of the earliest timbers were still in place. Facing north, they had been less susceptible than the other end of the house to centuries of rain blown in on the prevailing south-westerly wind. These wood-frame hall houses of Kent are really medieval prefabs, first assembled elsewhere with each timber marked with a Roman numeral. Contrary to legend, they were not built from the timbers of old warships, although in my own telephone box-sized hall there was a single piece of oak, possibly from the thirteenth century, that had obviously once been underwater.

Mainly my new home would have been constructed from the ancestors of the huge oak trees across the road that now sheltered it from the west wind, together with wattle and daub, Elizabethan bricks and soft sandstone from a quarry 100 yards away. The house had been assembled on sloping ground, creating a cellar at the north end, over which the wooden structure of the house was erected.

In over 500 years at least 100 people had lived in the house. Mysterious slots in the old timber, exposed for the first time for centuries by the modern builders, showed that cloth had once been woven in my new living room before being bleached and finished off in a field behind the house, and then stored in the cellar. Later, 'my' end, the north side of the house, had been one of many eighteenth-century beer houses. It also became obvious, as I began to test the soil and tune in for the first time to *Gardeners' Question Time*, that the contents of many centuries of heavily used privies lay beneath the surface. After battling with the builders' residue, I found that underneath the soil was so fertile that it could have been bagged up and sold at the front gate.

While I had immediately fallen in love with the view, I also began to enjoy my own little garden at the front of the cottage. Dog walkers, tramps and passing neighbours would all pause and call over the rickety fence as I struggled to return it to its original 'cottage garden' state.

'I'm afraid the garden is not looking its best yet,' I said to one of my new, and later, best neighbours.

'Oh, it's quite dreadful, dearie,' she replied. But she went on to give me lots of helpful advice, and she and her husband always called my garden 'Wannado' corner, because so many people would stop and say, 'Now what you wanna do is…' Others went further, especially an ancient neighbour who dropped an endless array of unidentifiable plants over the fence. 'More green stuff,' he would call, retreating before I could find out what the 'stuff' was.

As spring approached, I made my own first horticultural purchases: four tulips, which produced bright red and yellow heads which gave me immense pride and pleasure, but would never have won prizes at the flower show. I planted a cotoneaster to settle in and hide the drainage inspection tank at the back. It loved its new home and not only did the job, but also rapidly filled the whole of the small back garden. The other thing I planted, for sentimental reasons because I had actually moved into the house on Christmas Eve, was my first little Christmas tree. Right in the middle.

Now it was time to tackle the couch grass. I had always wanted to lay turf since as children my brother and I would open out our Swiss roll at teatime to lay chocolate lawns. But first the couch grass had to be eliminated, for which I needed the garden implement from hell – the rotavator. I was very short of money, so was delighted to be able to hire a machine for an absolute pittance. The owner seemed not to worry about when I might return it.

A huge rust-covered contraption, it leapt into life, with a roar that must have been audible across the county. I selected 'drive' and it shot forward immediately, subjecting the couch grass to a terrible fate. Briefly triumphant but increasingly blinded by a thick, blue haze and smoke pouring out of the machine's every orifice, I discovered as I careered non-stop around my plot how rough the ground actually was. It was only just possible to control the beast, but at least, I thought, I was 'digging for victory'. The garden was being resurrected.

One or two passers-by waved and a neighbour mouthed an inaudible message, but I dared not and did not stop until there was a loud clunk and a sort of minor explosion from the engine. In the healing stillness that followed and as the smoke cleared, it became obvious that this afternoon had been the rotavator's last stand. Its blades never turned again, and it was months before I could persuade the owner to remove it for decent burial. Yet, after that

hellish ten minutes, the soil had emerged as rich and dark and luxurious as I could have hoped for.

But as Liz, my wife-to-be, pointed out when she saw what I had done, all my mechanical gardening had achieved was to divide up the evil tendrils into a million new roots, all now lying in wait under the earth for the spring rain and sunshine to bring them back to life with much multiplied and fertilized vigour.

Months later, Liz moved in and took charge of the garden. Day after day, while I sat indoors scripting *Songs of Praise* hymns, happy and inspired by the most beautiful place I had ever lived in, Liz forked and dug out the couch grass and buttercups and bindweed root by root, in weary but not unhappy silence. The barren, no-man's land created by my 'rotavator afternoon' was slowly transformed as Liz worked her way along the 'sheep tracks' through the buttercup and couch, which I had made with the longed-for rolls of turf.

The straight concrete path was removed and replaced with winding brick, with thyme and sedum and violets planted in the cracks. We both liked the idea of nurturing herbs and dividing the space up into separate little plots. I wanted a cottage garden of the sort painted by the Victorian artist, Birket Foster, to illustrate his book *In Rustic Britain*. His quotation from the writer Washington Irving was exactly what I was after:

The great charm of English scenery is the moral feeling that seems to pervade it. It is associated in the mind with feelings of order, of quiet, of well-established principles, of hoary usage and revered custom.

Later that first year, as the infant garden prepared for its winter sleep and as I gathered up the leaves, the wind carried the sound of a band playing 'Abide with me', our first intimation of the village's Remembrance Day parade. We went up to watch as a small band, then a troop of scouts, followed by more than a dozen veterans, marched proudly with their flags into our parish church.

Slowly over the next ten years, the garden was to come to life under Liz's hand and eye. It took years of hard work to deliver the 'moral feeling', compared with which, sitting under the apple tree working out how TV cameras could illustrate the seed-time and harvest hymns for *Songs of Praise* was a doddle. As the hymn writer William Cowper wrote:

Gardens are not made by singing 'Oh, how beautiful!' and sitting in the shade.

I only quarrelled with Liz when she insisted that certain trees and plants had to be removed if other things were to have a chance of life. My investment in six cypressus leylandi, the last few remaining at a nursery on the brink of liquidation, proved unpopular with the new head gardener, as they took happily to our fine soil and grew daily by the foot in every direction. And after a year or two my dear little Christmas tree, which I must admit was now big enough to offer to Trafalgar Square, mysteriously disappeared when I was away filming one week.

My major responsibility was the care of the old hedge, filled with blackthorn and old-fashioned rambling roses bordering the ancient sunken lane at the side of our home. A thousand years ago, it was part of a drove road where once herds of cattle and swine had been driven across from the north-east of Kent into the High Weald. Even before the first Norman church was built here, monks had passed this way to worship God in the centre of our hilltop village. I always hoped that I might find a tiny pilgrim cross while clearing the debris from the hedge. Over the years, the road had sunk four or five feet below the level of the garden and as the bank fell away, I had high hopes. We found discarded eighteenth-century clay pipes and Victorian glass bottles, but nothing at all of the friars and travelling priests who had passed by while the weaver's house was being built as the Wars of the Roses came to an end.

We acquired another authentic feature for our traditional cottage garden when Liz bought some bantam hens with feathery legs. They were provided with a substantial hen house, and our whole garden, in which we set up low perches, became their 'run'. Several generations were born there. These usually gentle creatures were not over zealous with egg production, but they managed to live in harmony with our dog and Burmese cat, and by then the garden was so overflowing with plants and flowers, any damage they might have done went unnoticed. Each morning, the garden came to life at dawn as Sir Glyn, our longest-surviving cockerel, began to crow inside the hen house. Even though we had patient neighbours who fortunately were all early risers, we knew that the wake-up call would continue until one of us braved the elements to open the hen house door and let everybody out. Then one day, Sir Glyn fought his own War of the Roses around the garden with a younger relative, and sadly the old boy never recovered. We built a big funeral pyre for him in the garden, but after that we rather lost heart, and gave the rest of the roost away to neighbours. In any case, by then we knew we would soon be moving on ourselves.

The bantams and the little garden with the huge view were a great source of distraction and inspiration for both Liz and me over the ten years we lived there. By the end, we were working on rival religious programmes, for the BBC and ITV. I like to think that Dame Thora Hird's *Praise Be!* scripts for BBC ONE and Sir Harry Secombe's *Highway* for ITV benefited from being written across the same dining room table in such a beautiful place.

Now, 20 years on, passing our old home you can hardly see the garden. It has matured and blossomed and become hidden behind the hedgerows as if it were centuries old. The Remembrance parade goes on, but the men and women who sang 'Abide with me' that first year have long gone. All but one of the oak trees still provide shelter, and the ancient hedge still lurches along out into the old drove road. One day, a year or two after we had moved to Scotland, *Songs of Praise* came from our old village, and tears of happiness and regret were shed as two viewers recognized their own garden of Eden with its old apple tree where they had begun a new life together.

Kindly spring is here again,
trees and fields in bloom appear;
hark! The birds with artless lays
warble their creator's praise.

Where in winter all was snow
now the flowers in clusters grow
and the corn, in green array,
promises a harvest-day.

Lord, afford a spring to me,
let me feel like what I see;
speak, and by thy gracious voice,
make my drooping soul rejoice.

On thy garden deign to smile,
raise the plants enrich the soil;
soon thy presence will restore
life to what seemed dead before.
JOHN NEWTON (1725–1807)

(John Newton, once a slave trader, whose change of heart is described in his hymn 'Amazing Grace', wrote this hymn in 1779 when he left Olney to be vicar of a London church. In the Buckinghamshire village, Newton and his fellow hymn-writer William Cowper were inspired by the garden at Orchard Side, the vicarage where they both lived.)

Pilgrimage:
A Little Miracle in Lourdes

EASTERTIDE

Walk with me, O my Lord,
through the darkest night and brightest day
be at my side, O Lord,
hold my hand and guide me on my way.

ESTELLE WHITE (B. 1925)

It was a TV 'holiday programme' with a difference – *Songs of Praise* en fête is the best way to describe one of the series' rare visits to France. Diane Louise Jordan, along with the largest, jolliest children's pilgrimage in the world, was in Lourdes, where Roman Catholics and non-Catholics, young and old, were all brimming over with their enthusiastic impressions of the place:

'I believe something extraordinary happened here…'

'Even if it's the first time you've come here, after a few days you feel you've known everyone for years…'

'You can come here and look for the awful tackiness or you can come looking for the wonderfulness and the greatness…'

They had come to the place where in 1858 a sickly and simple 14-year-old peasant girl, Bernadette Soubirous, had told her family she had been talking to a beautiful woman, 'as young and small as herself', whom she had met when collecting firewood near the grotto. 'The lady' told Bernadette that her name was 'the Immaculate Conception', invited her to pray and later asked her to 'Go and tell the priests to come here in procession and build a chapel.'

Soon Bernadette was being followed to the grotto by crowds of people whenever she went to pray there, but nobody saw or heard anything other than a sudden calm happiness spread across the little girl's face.

Now, each year five million people from 150 countries come to this valley of south-eastern France, sheltered by the Pyrenees mountains. They come to the cave in the rock face, to pray where Bernadette prayed, and to wash in a spring of water that first appeared after Bernadette had spoken to 'the lady'.

Many come in physical and mental pain, praying that they might return home healed by a miraculous cure. Although the Roman Catholic church has only recognized about 60 healing miracles in the past 150 years, the visitor sees that there are many more than 60 pairs of crutches hanging from the rock face above the grotto. As Diane Louise Jordan said, at the end of her *Songs of Praise* pilgrimage, 'What goes on here cannot be answered in words alone, it has got to be seen.'

Just a week after Diane Louise had been in Lourdes with the *Songs of Praise* cameras, I went there myself. It was just after Easter 1996, and that Lent I had been responsible for making *Songs of Praise* for the saddest Mothering Sunday ever. We had gone to Dunblane, following the shooting of so many children and their teachers in the town's primary school. Many people in the wider community needed to share the sadness of everyone in that bereaved town, and we hoped that *Songs of Praise* would be a gentle way to allow this to happen. But anyone who was there at that time could not help but get caught up emotionally in the tragedy, and afterwards I very much needed to get right away. However, as a non-Roman Catholic, I was not expecting anything more from Lourdes than a short break in the spring sun.

I have a fairly open mind about the supernatural, and like a sizeable minority in Britain, I believe that I have seen a ghost, but my faith in religious apparitions has never been strong, ever since as a student visiting Edinburgh I was pursued along Princes Street by a man trying to sell me a piece of his wallpaper, on which he said the Virgin Mary regularly appeared. I became a little less sceptical in 1986, when the writer Ted Harrison and I made a film about a young English woman called Jane, who bore the stigmata, sores on her hands which bled and which she believed corresponded with the wounds in

Christ's hands on the cross. Jane's husband, a thoroughly down-to-earth man, believed her story, that she had been visited by the Virgin Mary in their council house living room. Like Bernadette's friends in Lourdes, he had not seen anything more than a serene expression on his wife's face, but he had felt a temperature change and there was a strong scent of flowers. It all sounded odd, and yet it had been strangely convincing, even to the sceptical film crew.

The first sight of the town of Lourdes confirms one's worse fears about religious commercialism, with crowds of souvenir shops lining both sides of the little streets. Here among the candles, rosaries, statues, vases and ashtrays and anything you can think of, was the 'illuminated Vatican', a music box sporting a different pope at each window. No doubt these shops will soon be offering the 'Jesus action figure with poseable arms and gliding action' that I spotted recently for sale in a bookshop in Scotland.

The first impression, however, is completely misleading. Down at the bottom of the town, the noisy, gaudy shops are left behind and replaced by open space, quiet and even austere, dominated by a large church built on a rocky outcrop. Here the loudest sound is birdsong, and the flapping of the flags of many nations. People have left bunches of flowers tied to the railings. Somewhere nearby is the grotto by the river where Bernadette came to gather firewood, but there are no signs to show you the way, and there is no admission charge. We will just follow the others, by day or by night.

The 1996 *Songs of Praise* from Lourdes marked the 40th anniversary of the Handicapped Children's Pilgrimage Trust, with 5,000 children with special needs who had set off from all over Britain and Europe on Easter Sunday for a huge musical celebration. When we arrived, a week later, some of the children, many living with severe physical and mental disability, were still there. When we entered the Basilica Church, which the 'beautiful young woman' had told Bernadette should be built, we found it was packed with happy children, many in wheelchairs. I never knew whether Suzi Hadlow, in her uncomfortable splints, was amongst them, but they all clearly shared the faith and energy which she had described with a mischievous smile to Diane Louise: 'I really love jumping up and down during mass… and I'm allowed to! But I go to pray especially for my grandfather who died of cancer. He's all right now – he's in heaven.

Sometimes I send him a balloon, and let it go so that it flies up to heaven.'

Our own rather more restrained little group of pilgrims from London was soon completely hemmed in by a singing, swaying and clapping choir in baseball caps, introducing us to Daniel O'Donnell's song *My Forever Friend*. That was the first blessing. As I became just a little less stiff-necked, I felt as though I was being welcomed back into the human race by these children. French and English blended as we all just kept singing on and on, with apparently no particular plan. A song from another great spiritual centre in France, Taizé, had even the 90-year-old in our party clapping along in rhythm.

In the Lord I'll be ever thankful;
In the Lord I will rejoice!
Look to God, do not be afraid,
Lift up your voices, the Lord is near.
Lift up your voices, the Lord is near.

O ma joie et mon espérance,
Le Seigneur est mon chant;
C'est de lui que vient le pardon,
En lui j'espère, je ne crains rien.
En lui j'espère, je ne crains rien.

CHANTS FROM TAIZÉ

This was the spirit of Lourdes, and I wanted to become a life member. Walking through the little town with my companions, we visited the poor little room in the Cachot where Bernadette and all her family had lived in extreme poverty, and then, passing a church nearby from where we could hear singing, we entered and stood quietly at the back to listen to a mass that was in progress. It was for children, and while the gospel was being read aloud, it was being acted out by children dressed as disciples. Jesus reached out to Doubting Thomas and put his hand to his sides with such sweetness and gentleness that it brought out all the emotional depth in the story, made all the more poignant because both Jesus and Doubting Thomas were in wheelchairs.

The next morning our group of six was back in the Basilica above the grotto. Like the medieval English cathedral before the Reformation, the big church is surrounded by tiny chapels, provided so that individual pilgrim groups can have their own services if, like us, they have a priest with them. As with many Lourdes features, we began by queuing in silence before moving into our own chapel. All along the corridor, the gentle sounds of whispered prayer in many different languages was explained by a little notice on the altar asking each priest, please, not to raise his voice.

By chance, we all chose to go separately to the place under the rock that has made Lourdes an international shrine to Our Lady. By contrast with the boisterous singing in the Basilica, I don't remember ever being in the middle of such a quiet and unthreatening crowd. At first I wondered where the grotto was, as everyone moved gently across a sort of parade ground, past rows of lighted candles and flowers left by earlier pilgrims. The crowd carried me slowly on past lines of covered wheelchairs, each with an attendant, waiting to be taken into the pool of water fed by Bernadette's spring. There were even candles adorned with the *Songs of Praise* logo, and then, when I found others inscribed, 'Remember the children of Dunblane', I realized that I was bringing my own story of Dunblane to a place made holy by a schoolchild.

I had no idea what to expect when, as part of this multitude of strangers, I found we had gradually organized ourselves into an orderly queue leading to the rock face.

In nineteenth-century Lourdes, under the cliff near the fast flowing Massabielle river, filled with the melting snows of the Pyrenees, there was unprepossessing, rough pasture where the town's pigs grazed. It would have been hazardous to reach, especially for little children sent there to gather wood, having to dodge the baleful gaze of a local mill owner who chased away trespassers. It was a dirty and scruffy place, and the cave in the rock had acquired the reputation of a place where evil spirits lurked. When Bernadette first told her family that she had seen and spoken to a small barefoot figure there a number of times, a *jeune fille* standing on a rock in the grotto near a wild rose bush, they were angry. Her teacher told her to stop her 'pranks'. When people started to follow Bernadette down to the grotto to see what happened, the police intervened to stop them. Bernadette stuck to her story, and even said she would take people's prayers to the grotto. While the church authorities scorned the poor, ignorant little girl, Lourdes itself was becoming famous as newspaper reporters descended on the town. Even her sceptical family noticed that Bernadette's chronic cough disappeared when she was kneeling close to the wild rose bush at the grotto's mouth. A small piece of the rose tree was placed around the neck of a dying baby, which immediately began to recover. The miracles of Lourdes had begun.

The grotto still looked very ordinary as I shuffled forward in line. The deep peacefulness made a far greater impression, as eventually my turn came to wend my way up a little concrete path under the overhanging rock, to pass a small statue of the Virgin Mary, and touch the water oozing from the rock. I was too prissy to do what others did, and kiss the rock. Seconds later, a few steps on, I was back on the parade ground. That was it. The spring that Bernadette had found seems to be no more than an oozing damp alcove.

Perhaps it was the quiet atmosphere of the place that made me linger, and uncharacteristically, to put away my camera. Suddenly, I did not want to leave the vicinity of that damp alcove above me. This meant a determined clamber through the wheelchairs and around kneeling pilgrims. I wanted my own patch of damp concrete. I'm not good at kneeling upright in church, and my 'holy' posture is a sort of crouch, leaning lazily against the pew in front. But on that chilly spring afternoon, I hardly noticed that a considerable time passed whilst I knelt bolt upright on the cold concrete ground. It was painless; it was also extraordinarily calming. My muddled, unhappy head seemed to clear. I have never been able to repeat the experience anywhere else since.

After dark that evening, we resumed our pilgrimage as a group and joined the nightly candlelight procession to the grotto – for the *jeune fille* had asked Bernadette Soubirous for there to be processions.

As we lit each other's candles, neatly packaged in holders on which were printed the words 'Ave Maria', the wind was rising. The process stopped and started as friendships were formed among strangers trying to keep each other's candles alight. We sang in a most un-*Songs of Praise* style, slowly circling the area, crossing and recrossing the waters of the Massabielle, ourselves a river of fluttering, guttering lights, until we ended up where we had begun. Yet we were not back where we had begun. In different ways Lourdes had changed us all, we had all moved on, and I had experienced my own small healing miracle at the grotto.

Like Kenny Williams, a fellow Scot who was interviewed on *Songs of Praise* from Lourdes, I am not a Roman Catholic. Kenny came as a volunteer after his severely disabled daughter died, 'to see what she had missed'.

I understood what he meant when, looking at hundreds of Roman Catholics, his new friends, he said, 'I'm probably getting more out of it than they are.'

The Queen's Birthday

● ● ● ● ● ● ● ● ● ● ● ● ● ● ●

Her Majesty has two birthdays. Her official birthday in June coincides with the brilliant ceremonial of the Trooping of the Colour in her presence on Horse Guards Parade in London, but her natural birthday is almost two months earlier.

On 21 April the church also commemorates St Anselm. Born in Italy in 1033, Anselm was a great traveller until he came to a complete halt at Bec in France, where he stayed and became a monk. After the Norman Conquest, and after 30 years of teaching, he was elected archbishop of Canterbury. Unlike his later successor, Thomas à Beckett, he died in 1109 of natural causes, but like Thomas he was sent into exile for displeasing the king with his preaching.

On 21 April 1979, I was producing *Songs of Praise* from St Michael's Church in Highgate. I always knew that my grandparents on my father's side had

been married there in 1906, but it was a coincidence to discover that this, my first and only visit to the church, was on what would have been their 73rd wedding anniversary.

I treasure a photograph taken when Tom and Evelyn were courting. My grandmother is enjoying her picnic in front of their Argyll motor car somewhere in the countryside. The car has no registration plate and so the picnic must have taken place in 1903, when these cars were the pride of Scotland's new motor industry. In later life, my father proudly showed the picture of the Argyll to a former employee of the firm, who replied, 'Aye, they were the world's worst.' Another employee, John Logie Baird, later invented television.

On the night of *Songs of Praise* in Highgate, as I remembered Tom and Evelyn, my ancestors, the congregation sang a hymn of praise, a setting of Psalm 103, so often chosen for services attended by Her Majesty the Queen.

Praise, my soul, the King of heaven,
to his feet thy tribute bring.
Ransomed, healed, restored, forgiven,
who like me his praise should sing?
Praise him! Praise him!
Praise him! Praise him!
Praise the everlasting King!
HENRY LYTE (1793–1847)

St George's Day

23 APRIL

Flag officers – many parish churches in England have them – will have left their beds early today to ensure that a white flag emblazoned with a red cross is flying from the top of the tower to celebrate England's patron saint, St George. The proper procedure is to haul it up at first light on 23 April, not a second sooner, and then lower it at dusk. When I was made a church warden in Kent, I always took my duty very seriously, setting two alarms and falling sleepily out of bed in the false dawn that precedes sunrise in the countryside in order to be the one to raise the flag.

I was nearly always thwarted. My nimble-footed senior colleague always managed to race up the tower's hundred steps and set the standard flying seconds before I arrived, although he lived outside the village. Once we fought a friendly duel with our church keys to unlock the tiny medieval door at the top of the tower and be first to the pole.

It may sound like a pointless and silly contest, but there was something very moving about raising the saint's flag to fly proudly over the landscape of the High Weald of Kent. From the tower in Goudhurst we could see almost two dozen other parish churches, and my competitiveness extended to taking a pair of binoculars with me to see if we were first to proclaim the good news of the festival day to England.

St George does not have the same status in the Roman Catholic Church, and the saint's demotion by the Vatican 20 years ago raised eyebrows in the English shires. St George is the patron of the most noble Order of the Garter, commemorated in the spectacularly beautiful surroundings of the Queen's Free Chapel of St George in Windsor Castle. He is believed to have been a soldier living in Palestine who was martyred for his faith early in the fourth century. He is usually depicted wearing armour, but historians say that the story of the slaying of the dragon is a myth.

Apart from scouring the Kentish countryside for flags on 23 April, we also used to search the sky for the first swallows and house martins. Many people know that it must be St George's Day when the first delicate little swallow is spotted balancing with the aid of its elegant long tail on a power line. In Scotland, the swallows sometimes arrive a day or so later. By one of the miracles of nature, these tiny birds, who winter thousands of miles to the south in the African Sahara, find their way back year after year to our old stable. They confidently reclaim their home in the rafters and soon begin to build their nests. We feel it is a great honour, and from now until September, we never enter the stable without asking their permission, and risk being dive-bombed, especially when it becomes a swallow nursery and flying lessons are underway.

We feel very blessed.

Swallow Poem

O Master masons of the Gothic churches,
Curb your pride!
You needed quadrants, rarely chiselled stones,
Pilasters, shafts and capitals and painted glass.
Your mortar was
The misery of multitudes who spent themselves
To dedicate your pile
To worlds to come,
To Death.

But see the swallows:

From dust and slime, from blades of grass and horsehair,
Religiously they build their vaulted nest,
And dedicate it
To this earth,
To Life.

FROM *THE SWALLOW BOOK*, WRITTEN BY ERNST TOLLER (1893–1939) IN PRISON IN 1923,
WHO DESCRIBED HOW HE SHARED HIS CELL WITH TWO SWALLOWS. TR. ASHLEY DUKES

Two Men in the Marsh

● ● ● ● ● ● ● ● ● ● ● ● ● ●

ROGATION SUNDAY

Rogation is derived from the Latin word *rogare*, meaning 'to ask'. It is observed widely in Catholic Europe, and in the Church of England on the fifth Sunday after Easter. Based on what was once a pagan custom, many rural congregations leave their churches and go in procession out to the fields where new crops are growing, to pray for a good harvest for their community. In the topsy-turvy world of sixteenth-century England, such processions were first of all banned, and then made compulsory in Queen Elizabeth the First's reign. The 1662 *Book of Common Prayer* prescribes three full days of fasting to follow Rogation Sunday.

Standing in a tiny church in the middle of a marsh as my film crew and I prepared to record Robert Bridge's Rogation hymn, 'Rejoice O land, in God thy might', I realized that probably no one had ever attempted it here before, and certainly not with the famous hymn-writer, Sydney Carter, and the broadcaster and journalist, Malcolm Muggeridge, TV's 'St Mugg', among the choir of angelic voices. This was Rogation Sunday 1987, and the hymn writer and the journalist were being filmed on a walk together through the Romney Marshes, visiting old churches and reflecting on the state of Christianity in the last years of the twentieth century.

M.M. DRAWN BY EMILIO COIA

Rejoice, O land, in God thy might,
his will obey, him serve aright;
for thee the Saints uplift their voice:
fear not, O land, in God rejoice.

Glad shalt thou be, with blessing crowned,
with joy and peace thou shalt abound;
yea, love with thee shall make his home
until thou see God's kingdom come.

He shall forgive thy sins untold:
remember thou his love of old;
walk in his way, his word adore,
and keep his truth for evermore.
ROBERT BRIDGES (1844–1930)

I had wanted to make a full-length film with Malcolm Muggeridge since my earliest days in television, having spent many months with him when I was first learning to be a researcher and to direct cameras. His 'live' Sunday night programme, *The Question Why*, was my baptism of fire, but it was made far easier for me by the presenter. Malcolm was always a consummate professional in the medium which, with wit and not a little wisdom, he never ceased to despise. But in 1987, when the filmed walk was proposed, some people thought I had left it too late.

'St Mugg', by then in his early 80s, still had the piercing bright eyes that had been used to such effect during his inquisitorial Sunday broadcasts from the BBC's Lime Grove studios. The man whose faith had been awakened by his encounter with Mother Teresa at her 'House of the Dying' in Calcutta, was untroubled by the peculiar rituals of television production, but increasing difficulties with hearing and eyesight were bothering him. I should perhaps have paid more attention to the experiences of Liz, my wife, who only a few years before had produced *Home on Sunday* with his wife, the Madonna-like Kitty Muggeridge. Arriving at Park Cottage in Robertsbridge, the much-visited place of pilgrimage for Muggeridge devotees and TV crews, Kitty had warmly welcomed Liz with the words, 'We are so happy to see you in our home, but please don't mind if in a few minutes we can't remember who you are.'

Characteristically, Malcolm had emerged from meditation with his much-beloved *Book of Common Prayer* to announce that he had nothing to say, but had then gone on to contribute at great length in Kitty's interview with Cliff Michelmore. The man who had by turns stimulated and antagonized millions of viewers might have become the Methuselah of TV, but he was still game to broadcast – and we were still all knocking on his door.

I had always admired Sydney Carter for his almost revolutionary Christian songs that had chimed with my own mildly rebellious student days of the 1960s. Paying tribute to his father on *Songs of Praise*, shortly after his death in 2004, Mike Carter said that Sydney liked to describe himself as a 'doubting Christian songwriter'. At our initial meeting, Sydney revealed that he too was suffering from a cataract, but he was full of ideas for the walk through the Marshes with Malcolm, and he promised to bring a small drum with which he could accompany any singing they might do to keep their spirits up.

The weather was perfect when the crew arrived at Fairfield for the first day's filming. Fortunately, the tiny church of St Thomas à Beckett, which sits in the middle of a field, was no longer surrounded by flood water, as it had been when I made my site visit. Now, in the afternoon sunshine, Christians from many of the Marshes' parishes would soon fill the field, processing into the church for their annual Rogationtide service, where Malcolm and Sydney would join them. I hoped that Sydney would find here a sign of hope to balance Malcolm's well-known theory that the Anglican church was in terminal decline. Yet with 15 minutes to go, there was no sign of anyone to join the inquisitive sheep peering at our camera. No processing Christians, no Malcolm, no Sydney. Was Malcolm to win his argument before we had even begun?

Sydney Carter seemed to materialize from nowhere – in fact from behind a disused barn – hailing me as if I were a complete stranger, with an urgent request for a loo. It was an enormous relief to see him, and to arrange for his relief by knocking on the door of the only house for miles, where a kindly but startled family was in the middle of lunch. The question was, how had Sydney, who did not drive, got to this place in the middle of nowhere? When he emerged, he told me cheerfully that he had followed my instructions to the letter and got off the train at the terminus where he was to be met. As no one was there, he had hailed a taxi. Then he added, 'The taxi man is here, waiting behind the barn; can you settle up?'

He was right. Behind the barn, a cabbie, smiling as his meter continued to clock up a fare in excess of £50, could not believe his luck. He had driven across two counties from the wrong terminus to which Sydney had travelled in the wrong train, and so enjoyed an unexpected excursion.

Returning to the crew, much the poorer, I found that there was still no sign of any Rogationtide Christians, but Malcolm had arrived, driven by his good friend Geoffrey, who, for which I was to be for ever grateful, had been endowed with an unshakeable sense of humour and optimism. It was to preserve me in the filming days ahead.

I shall never know whether in spite of the description of their being 'very old friends', the two had, in fact, ever set eyes on each other before. Malcolm smiling, but particularly gnomic, seemed happy enough to stand in the sun with his new acquaintance, 'Yes, I've heard a lot about you,' he said, but clearly wondered what more was to happen other than this pleasant chance encounter.

With five minutes to go, I still needed to solve the mystery of the missing Rogation procession, as it was clear that everyone was beginning to wonder if we were *all* in the wrong place. Hoping my rising panic wasn't too evident, I tried to look nonchalant as I walked away from Malcolm and Sydney in the

direction of an unpromising farm building. Carried by a gust of wind, I had thought I had heard a snatch of the hymn 'Rejoice, O land, in God thy might'. The singing stopped. I was beginning to fear that I was hallucinating, until I turned a corner of the barn into a completely different world.

Surrounded by hay bales, the local vicar, the late Tony Towse, was standing arrayed in a fine golden cape of the sort usually seen in cathedral worship. To this day, I cannot work out how they had got there without any of us seeing them – a man robed in white carrying a cross, church wardens with their staves, hymn books and even a portable lectern. I could have hugged them all with relief, but Anglican reticence prevailed.

The vicar was mid-sermon, being listened to attentively by a sizeable gathering. 'Is our Rogation procession something we should be doing?' he was asking as I arrived. 'Or is it an excuse for a picnic and a charade, hoping people won't laugh at us?' I just hoped the question was rhetorical, because I for one very much needed them to be doing it.

Back in the fields surrounded by wildly leaping lambs, Malcolm and Sydney were getting acquainted. The dramatis personae were all now in place for the film, but we only had one camera, and I needed to show the procession as well as see Malcolm and Sydney talking about it simultaneously. I persuaded Tony Towse and his faithful congregation to remain concealed in their barn a little while longer. Meanwhile, Sydney and Malcolm, following a film convention that I knew was in 'St Mugg's' blood, would talk about the procession as though it was passing in front of them – even though it hadn't actually started yet. It is the only way, as everyone who has been interviewed for *Songs of Praise* will know, to film in two opposite directions at once with a single camera.

I led Malcolm and Sydney a little way along a sheep track. Then I went back to stand with the camera, and at my signal they began to walk towards us, to talk about the invisible procession. 'Yes,' said Malcolm, his eyes glinting with his accustomed professionalism, 'but did you know this church has been moved?'

Sydney looked bemused. 'Well, yes, but it seems a bit odd they've brought it to the middle of nowhere.'

'Yes, but in spite of that,' said Malcolm, 'it's a lesson for other churches; they might take heart from what's happened here.'

Although a Quaker, Sydney was an admirable sparring partner for Malcolm. Malcolm, as ever was utterly convincing. Although very deaf and almost blind, he was sometimes forgetful, but not, I believe, senile. In his old age he was still revelling in mocking what he called the 'utter absurdity' of TV, and the complacent assumptions of film makers, while losing none of his own professionalism.

He conspired with us on another day, when he was feeling unwell, by allowing the production assistant to don his coat and cap and, adorned with a wispy, white wig, to shuffle gently across the landscape with an utterly unfazed Sydney.

The journey could not be contemplated, Malcolm said to Sydney, without a visit to his oldest friend, Dr Alec Vidler, with whom years before Malcolm had fought six terrific rounds as the two men were filmed on another journey, *In the Steps of St. Paul*. The conversation in Dr Vidler's Rye home began with the mystery of the moving church.

'The fact that these churches were built where there was no population bears reflection,' said Dr Vidler enigmatically.

Malcolm, determined to regain the upper hand by changing tack altogether, replied, 'I often think first-century saints would have been dumbfounded if they found themselves at Evensong; remember, Paul was the originator of Christianity and that is something, isn't it?'

The filming was frequently interrupted by the antics of a huge tabby cat who moved from one lap to another, and eventually terminated when the equally forgetful Dr Vidler forgot we were all there and wandered off to listen to his radio.

Always blessed by the kindly spring sun, Malcolm and Sydney, two men in a marsh, crossed and recrossed the flat Kent landscape, deep in conversation. While Malcolm was ruminating on death and old age one afternoon, Sydney confessed, 'The prayer book talks about "the shades lengthening, the busy world is hushed and our work is done…" He expostulated, 'But my work *isn't* done! I've still so much that I haven't yet done!'

In our separate lives of procrastination and distraction, the crew and I knew only too well what he meant.

In St Augustine's, Snave, a church long ago declared redundant, Malcolm and Sydney quizzed the new owner, who had campaigned to stop the church being turned into a house because he didn't want a cesspool installed where his ancestors were buried. He pointed out to them that having the church full for an annual service at harvest time would have been exactly how the church was in medieval times, rather than a weekly country congregation of two or three.

They visited St Dunstan's, Snargate, once home to Barham, the author of the *Ingoldsby Legends*, who had written, 'The world is divided into four parts – Europe, Africa, Asia and Romney Marsh.'

Sydney inspected a brass memorial plate to a former vicar, reading out his many academic qualifications. 'Yes, but that's highly suspicious,' barked

Malcolm instantly, 'Jesus had no degrees; he didn't even write a book. He just had wise sayings.'

All that was left of Hope All Saints were three forlorn pillars in a field, the decay being hastened by a rising gale. 'It reminds me of a visit to the dentist,' said Sydney, inspecting the jagged stumps. 'Hope,' said Malcolm, 'scarcely exists; faith would be a better word.'

Over the weeks, as they moved slowly from one ancient church to another, glancing briefly at the passing scene, Malcolm pursued his own last testament, from a text provided by another friend, Archbishop Fulton Sheen from the U.S.A., that 'Christendom is over – but not Christ.'

This programme, described by one TV critic as one of the most eccentric portraits of England of all time, was to be Malcolm's last. For me, the experience was by turns an alarming, hilarious and yet deeply moving portrait not just of old age but of the everlasting spirit of enquiry. The old Marsh churches and the two companions walking from one to the other in the afternoon spring sunshine helped me glimpse an eternal landscape.

At the end, joined by Kitty Muggeridge, Malcolm and Sydney found themselves at Evensong in Brookland Church, where the same Tony Towse who had welcomed them to Fairfield, preached on the theme, 'The only hindrances to Christianity: the church, the Bible and the prayer book.' I noticed Malcolm swiftly turning down his hearing aid immediately after the Nunc Dimittis. Like Counsel prosecuting his case, he had concluded 'no more questions'.

'Tis the gift to be simple, 'tis the gift to be free,
'tis the gift to come down where you ought to be
and when we find ourselves in the place just right,
'twill be in the valley of love and delight.

When true simplicity is gained,
to bow and to bend we shan't be ashamed;
to turn, turn will be our delight,
till by turning, turning we come round right.
SIMPLE GIFTS, SHAKER SONG (C. 1837)

Don't Give Up!

• • • • • • • • • • • • • •

ASCENSION DAY

Hail the day that sees him rise, Alleluia!
to his throne beyond the skies; Alleluia!
Christ, awhile to mortals given, Alleluia!
enters now the highest heaven. Alleluia!

CHARLES WESLEY (1707–88)

One summer afternoon in 1915, an elderly lady had an unusual experience at her local church. Firstly, she had had to queue for two and a half hours to get in through the doors and then, she claimed in her letter of protest to her vicar, in the crush that followed her hat flew away and her umbrella was completely destroyed. Worst of all, as all the seats were immediately taken before she could find one, she was swept back out into the street and missed the service. She demanded compensation from the new vicar whose presence had caused the stampede. The new vicar sympathized and treasured the letter until he died.

DICK SHEPPARD

There must have been quite a revolution when Dick Sheppard, later to be the BBC's first radio 'personality', first arrived to be the new vicar at St Martin's in the Field in 1914. His 'goings-on', as they were described, included the introduction of weekday services, and the handsome church, a London landmark on the edge of Trafalgar Square, being kept open all hours. In wartime London, another elderly parishioner told Sheppard, 'What with air raids outside the church and you inside, there seems to be nothing but explosions.'

Soldiers returning from the battlefields of France came in mud-stained to pray in thanksgiving for their safe return, while others knelt there before crossing the road to board a troop train from Charing Cross Station and leave England, many of them for the last time.

It was a stroke of luck for radio listeners that in 1923 Randall Davidson, the archbishop of Canterbury, introduced John Reith, the BBC's first Director General, to Dick Sheppard. In 1924, the by now enormous regular congregation in St Martin's were joined by a far larger, unseen congregation listening at home. Broadcasts from St Martin's were an immediate hit with listeners who, far from staying away from church, swelled the queues to be in the congregation. Hundreds of letters were sent to the man with the sympathetic voice on the radio, who seemed so aware of all their needs and fears.

BISHOP JIM CELEBRATES

Sheppard, like many of his listeners in post-war England, was himself fighting against depression and ill health. His strength lay in his gift of empathy, and a willingness to draw on his own experience. He also understood the power of the new medium to link his inner-city congregation to the most isolated rural cottage and was able to address both. 'Beauty does not go with loneliness, and the vision of nature at her fairest is ghastly when one is unhappy and alone.'

Even before Reith introduced him to radio broadcasting, Dick Sheppard had already begun to broadcast through the telephone network. In the early days, the telephone companies were able to connect subscribers to theatres and churches. A microphone was installed in the pulpit and Sheppard was one of the successful London preachers who were hooked up. He also used it to great effect to comfort sick people who had written to him. While the choir was singing or the organ playing, he would lean into the microphone and, speaking gently, name the listeners who had written in, and add words of encouragement like: 'Don't give up!' or 'We are praying for you.'

In 2003, 80 years after Dick Sheppard's first broadcast on 2LO, the BBC's London radio station, another great crowd was pushing up the steps towards the classic portico of St Martin's in the Field for one of the most popular services on Radio 4 every year. It was Ascension Day and the London rush hour was at its peak as the pews filled just as they must have done in Sheppard's day. The Ascension Day Evening Service, broadcast 'live', is an annual highlight for listeners to Radio 4's *Daily Service* and gives them a rare opportunity to put faces to familiar voices, to see some of the regular singers normally based in Manchester, and to take part in the broadcast themselves.

As we rehearsed in the dim evening light in St Martin's, it was easy, unlike on *Songs of Praise* with its batteries of lights and cameras, to forget the technical complexities of broadcasting. Standing at the microphone, the present vicar, the Reverend Nick Holtam, with members of his clergy team and another well-known radio voice, the Reverend Angela Tilby, each rehearsed their contribution in turn to ensure that the broadcast timings were correct to the split second. Unlike the razzmatazz of television, the radio producer spoke quietly to each contributor, allowing the congregation their own thoughts and prayers as we prepared for the service to begin. However, before that it was our turn in the congregation to rehearse, a practice that was so unusual in 1924 when Dick Sheppard introduced it for the very first time, that it was reported in *Wireless World*. We all stood up to sing and were exhorted to emphasize our consonants and avoid the hissing 'sss' dreaded by radio producers. It was very hard work as the *Daily Service* audience found itself becoming the *Daily Service* choir.

The highlight of the broadcast was the sermon for Ascension Day, preached from the carved, wooden pulpit that is tall and rather creaky – a real radio hazard. However, the man in the pulpit was a highly skilled and greatly loved broadcaster, Bishop Jim Thompson, who was accustomed to much worse hazards in his regular *Thought for the Day* 'live' broadcasts from unattended BBC studios, from 'radio' cars and once even from a telephone box when a traffic jam had prevented him reaching the studio on time. His Ascension Day sermon was, as so often, made compelling by reflections on faith in the light of his own questioning spirit, a gift he shared with Dick Sheppard. We could not know as he spoke to us and to the invisible audience at home, that it was to be his last broadcast. A few weeks later, Bishop Jim died suddenly at sea.

I shall best remember Bishop Jim for a television contribution he made one Christmas Day in the 1980s. At the time, he was bishop of Stepney in East London and was proud that the BBC's new soap opera *EastEnders* was set in his diocese. 'Walford is part of our territory,' he said, before going on, 'All races in all time have searched for God. If we watch the sunrise and see it touch all living creatures with beauty, God is there. And in the eyes of the suffering child, God is there. There is nothing quite as dependent as a baby, if you think about it. Jesus was always dependent and rather powerless whilst he lived on earth. Some of you at home may feel vulnerable and afraid too. I wonder, how can one person, I or you, be significant? The Christmas message gives us the answer: the God, who was big enough to make the whole universe, was big enough to come to earth, to come for each one of us.'

After the Ascension Day Service, as Bishop Jim prepared for the long journey back to his home on Exmoor, he said to me, with characteristically modest diffidence, 'Was that all right?'

Yes, Bishop Jim, it was. You helped us all find new meaning and to see ourselves and our own lives in the story of Jesus being taken up into heaven, just as you once pointed to the significance of the night he was born in the stable. And I am sure that for all of us who were with him for that final broadcast, there is no doubt that Bishop Jim has joined the God who was big enough to make him.

There we shall with thee remain, Alleluia!
partners of thine endless reign; Alleluia!
there thy face unclouded see, Alleluia!
find our heaven of heavens in thee, Alleluia!
CHARLES WESLEY (1707–88)

SUMMER:
JUNE TO SEPTEMBER

To Colombo with Compline

* * * * * * * * * * * * * *

SUMMER
Before the ending of the day,
Creator of the world, we pray
that with thy wonted favour thou
wouldst be our guard and keeper now.

COMPLINE HYMN (7TH CENTURY OR EARLIER)

Two hours after the elderly Aeroflot jet left Moscow, 'the vicar, the churchwarden and his wife', seated in a row, began their evening worship. With only one copy of the traditional service of Compline between us, it had to be prayer hugger-mugger style as we strained our eyes to read the words by the low cabin light. Our row of three rather tatty seats had become a tiny outpost of the diocese of Canterbury.

This was before the days of Perestroika, and the cabin crew, who were all large and silent, would have made ideal extras in a James Bond movie. They eyed us suspiciously as they passed, or perhaps they were merely puzzled as to why three of their passengers had their heads together and were muttering in low voices in Shakespearean English. Never before had the service taken such a meaning, at least for Liz and me.

Above our heads, primitive air conditioning puffed clouds of steam downward, lending even more the impression that this was an 007 scenario. Underneath our feet and far below us was – where, and what? My geography failed, and it could have been the Russian Steppes, the Black Sea or the deserts of Asia for all I knew. But we prayed that the Creator would be 'our guard and keeper' that night, so that we might see a new day dawn in our destination, the beautiful island in the Indian Ocean, Sri Lanka.

It had all begun with the friendship between a Church of England vicar in South London and his Sri Lankan curate. After Bob Campbell-Smith moved as vicar to our country parish in Kent, he was encouraged to visit Sri Lanka for himself, and I think he had an inkling that what he found there might wake up some of his sleepy new rural parishioners. We in turn could perhaps offer support to the small Anglican population in a country that is predominantly Hindu and Buddhist in its religious beliefs.

'Nothing could have prepared me for the experience when I first went there in 1986,' he told me, 'so I wanted a small group of our parishioners to come and see for themselves.' In 1987 seven of us prepared to join him in what our Sri Lankan hosts called 'Father Bob's second missionary journey'.

The only problem about our visiting the paradise island, one of those idyllic faraway destinations of the television holiday programmes, was that an extremely nasty civil war was raging. Even the most insular British papers were recording the terrorist activities of the 'Tamil Tigers' and the militant JVP, the representatives of a small but violent minority of guerrillas hidden among the Hindu Tamil and Buddhist Sinhala communities, who had lived together in peace for centuries. Now they were killing each other. In the middle of all this carnage was our destination, the small Protestant theological college at Pilamatalawa near the old city of Kandy in the heart of Sri Lanka, where both Tamil and Sinhala students lived under one roof, training to be priests and ministers, with Anglicans, Methodists and Baptists all learning together.

It was alarming and sounded too much like the situation in Northern Ireland, as it was then, for our comfort, particularly as four of our party were teenagers. Much of the preparation took place in our cottage, since the vicarage telephone was on the blink and so Bob came round at all sorts of hours to try to speak to the college via the equally primitive Sri Lankan telephone system. As we watched his efforts to get information, our admiration for his quite saintly persistence increased, but Liz and I were increasingly in two minds. When he did get through, it was to a series of friendly but vague college administrators, who gave him no clue as to what might be going on. Yes, we were expected, but was it yesterday? Yes, there was a curfew, but only after dark. To go, or not to go, that was the question. Liz's diary:

Monday. We seem to be getting closer and closer to going to Sri Lanka – and I don't think it's going to be cancelled. The vicar seems hell-bent on going, and so does

Andrew. So I suppose we will go. I do hope we are not all hacked to death with axes while travelling by bus.

A few days later, we were off. To save money, we flew via Moscow and Bombay, courtesy of the old communist airline Aeroflot. By lunchtime the next day, we caught our first glimpse of Sri Lanka. The lush green forests, palm trees and sandy beaches we could see from the air looked like Robert Louis Stevenson's *Treasure Island*, an almost uninhabited landscape appearing to welcome us in peace.

On the ground, we were introduced to all the noise, heat and excitement of the Indian subcontinent, and to the strangely cheerful face of unconcealed poverty, and to what was to become our new rhythm of life. First we would shake hands with our ever-smiling hosts, then we would wait about, without evident purpose, until suddenly we would be moved off into frenzied activity. Bob Campbell-Smith's friend and former curate, Rienzi Perera, was the master of ceremonies, marching ahead calling imperiously: 'Come! come! come!' and

compressing our small party from Kent, together with our massive luggage, into a succession of small camper vans.

Another extract from Liz's diary:

Saturday. The last part of our journey from Colombo to Kandy was like taking part in a peculiarly dangerous stunt for some film. There was not enough room for all of us, so two of us had to sit among the cases in the back. Bob and Rienzi sat in comfort in the front seats – which is the tradition here: priests first, men second, women and children last. Andrew sat in the middle with Matthew and Katy, and Oliver (the vicar's son) and I crouched in the back for a three-hour journey of intense concentration by our driver.

Our Sri Lankan driver drove flat out and furiously along roads lined with graceful pedestrians and tables of coconuts. He carved an erratic course through ox carts, flimsy scooter taxis and huge trucks. We passed elephants sauntering along, unmoved by our high-pitched horn, which meant: 'I am not stopping – get into the ditch!' We ourselves gave way reluctantly and only to much bigger buses coming equally furiously towards us. We never hit anything, but the duel of horns was deafening. I soon discovered that the floor of the van was the safest place to be. Meanwhile, in a quiet matter-of-fact tone, Bob gave us a running commentary of the sights the quick-eyed might just glimpse as we whirled by. Sometimes we would come to a sudden complete halt and emerge past the smoking tyres to be introduced to a tea factory or a wayside stall selling fruit.

(After two such journeys, Liz said: 'Bob, where do you think Jesus would be sitting in this bus?' In spite of her protests that she was only teasing, Bob climbed in the back with her and Oliver for the rest of our time there.)

On our first morning in Sri Lanka, we awoke to a dawn cacophony of tropical bird shrieks and monkey calls. Throbbing drums sounded out across the valley from a Buddhist temple above the college. Outside our window was a banana tree covered in fruit. The students from the college, all handshakes and smiles, appeared, and each one of us was individually greeted. Then we sat cross-legged on the floor of the chapel in the theological college and sang 'Praise to the Lord, the Almighty, the King of creation' by the seventeenth-century European teacher Joachim Neander. It felt odd indeed to be singing so familiar a song in this strange land.

Clearly, the kingdom they were praying for would be a courteous and hospitable place. Since we were surrounded with such kindness and faith, we had no fear while we were there, even at night when young soldiers checked us in the pitch dark after the curfew time.

Every time – and there were a great many times, in churches, houses and once even in a jungle clearing – that we joined Sri Lankans to sing and pray, we noticed the impact of language. When the worship was in Sinhala, people chose to sit together, but if the service was in English, they scattered about like Anglican church congregations in England. When the hymns were from Victorian England, they were sung very properly, but when the choruses were in Sinhala, the voices became passionate and intense. There was not the flamboyance of a gospel choir, but even without translation, the singing left no doubt that we were with people who felt the presence of God.

In the cathedral in Kurunagula, the organist spotted us and came over to apologize for losing her place in the tune 'Evelyns' as we sang 'At the name of Jesus' from Miss Caroline Noel's nineteenth-century hymnal for invalids. 'Some of us were brought up in the colonial days and we can't give up the old hymns. It's wrong, but...'

Songs of Praise will probably never come from Sri Lanka and now, almost 20 years after our own visit, the Anglican hymns have all but vanished as Sri Lanka's next generation of Christians have found the confidence to worship in their own Tamil and Sinhalese tongues. The Buddhist custom of chanting seems natural here, though the content is Christian. And their Christian faith is enriched when the teaching of the 'Triple Refuge' – Buddha, teaching and community – transforms so naturally into the triple nature of God: Father, Son and Holy Spirit.

Sri Lanka is now in the daily prayers of Goudhurst, a village that once saw hop pickers from Bermondsey as 'foreigners'. Together with neighbouring Kilndown, there is regular contact and funding for pre-school activities and the running of a rubber plantation to maintain the church in the village of

Molkawa. A new tea plantation is being established to help the people of an isolated church in Urrubokke, and the Bishop of Colombo's work to reopen links with the once besieged Tamil city of Jaffna is being funded.

Goudhurst benefits from regular visits from their far-away neighbours. The Reverend Kerti Fernando and his wife June have been there. She taught songs and dances to the village primary school while he worked at the University of Kent. Even in my own time as churchwarden, the choir learnt a Sinhala Communion setting, so that we could make our visitors as welcome as they once made us, on the day after we had wobbled nervously through Compline in the communist airliner. Now Goudhurst has become a tiny part of the Diocese of Colombo.

O Father, that we ask be done
through Jesus Christ, thine only Son;
who, with the Holy Ghost and thee
doth live and reign eternally. Amen.
COMPLINE HYMN (7TH CENTURY OR EARLIER)

Sing a New Song

WHITSUNTIDE

The day of Pentecost had come, and they were all together in one place. Suddenly there came from the sky what sounded like a strong, driving wind, a noise which filled the whole house where they were sitting. And there appeared to them flames like tongues of fire distributed among them and coming to rest on each one. They were all filled with the Holy Spirit and began to talk in other tongues, as the Spirit gave them power of utterance.

ACTS 2:1–4

W atching the now annual *Songs of Praise – School Choir of the Year* finals, and sharing in the pleasure of seeing choirs from Northern Ireland make a clean sweep in 2004, brought back memories of another *Songs of Praise* competition from 1985, in search of the best new hymn writing. More than 500 people of all ages entered, and Sally Magnusson introduced the eight winners in St James's Church, Piccadilly, talking to each writer before an enthusiastic congregation tried out their hymns.

Miss Violet Barnett from Weymouth had drawn on her long career in teaching to write, with children's voices in mind, 'Loving Father, hear our song.'

'I don't know what the recipe for success is, but with a cheerful tune and comforting words, that *might* be all right.' Miss Barnett, like her fellow composers, had to wait until her grilling from Sally was over before she could hear her hymn sung for the first time, by a children's choir from Furzedown School:

Loving Father, hear our song
singing, singing,
keep us safe the whole day long
in your loving care.

When everyone in the congregation joined in, it was obvious her instinct was correct.

For his colleagues in religious broadcasting, it was a surprise that a hymn written by Peter Brooks was one of the eight winners. Peter, although credited literally hundreds of times over the years as 'Television Producer R.T. Brooks', before he retired had never had any connection with *Songs of Praise*. To ensure that the judging was scrupulously impartial, the judges, chaired by hymn-writer Cyril Taylor, had been given no more than a code to identify each entry. So all that they knew as they picked the hymn 'Spirit of God', was that it was written by 'A4'.

'A4' had chosen Hubert Parry's tune 'Intercessor' to go with the words. As he said to Sally on the night, 'Because it suits words which are about both praise and confession. The words "Spirit of God", which begin each verse, lead on to acknowledge adoration for all God gives us, contrasted with our confession that we are so slow to receive.'

He also confessed that he had only previously written three hymns in 40 years, a strike rate of a new work every 20 years. 'This competition jerked me into a rush to finish one in five years.'

Peter died a few months later. His winning hymn is simple and beautiful, although it has never achieved the popularity of his 'Thanks to God whose word was spoken', which ensured Peter's place in the *Songs of Praise* hymnbook.

I remember thinking that it was characteristic of Peter's reticent personality that when his hymn was sung, the lights were lowered to create an atmosphere of prayer, with the lights of nearby Piccadilly coming through the windows to cast a pattern of light on the beautiful Wren ceiling of the nave.

Spirit of God

Spirit of God, in all that's true I know you;
yours is the light that shines through thoughts and words.
Forgive my mind, slow as it is to read you,
my mouth so slow to speak the truth you are.

Spirit of God, in beauty I behold you;
yours is the loveliness of all that's fair.
Forgive my heart, slow as it is to love you,
my soul so slow to wonder at your grace.

Spirit of God, in all that's good I meet you;
yours is the rightness in each deed of love.
Forgive my will, slow as it is to serve you,
my feet so slow to go, my hands to do.

Spirit of God, in Jesus Christ you find me;
in Him you enter through the door of faith.
From deep within me, take possession of me –
my will, my heart, my mind all matched to his.
R.T. BROOKS (1918–85)

SONGS OF PRAISE FROM HADDINGTON

Beginning with an Empty Page

Writing is a compulsion, but I dread it and fear it. At first, until you fill it, it is just you and the empty page.

JOHN RUTTER (B. 1945)

I have always been fascinated by this image of an artist beginning with a blank page, before going on to create something that may change the whole world's understanding of itself. It would be ludicrously grandiose to link this with my own new, late in life, writing career, but because I have to get up each morning and turn ideas into words – at least I now know something about dread and fear and the empty page.

The artist rarely lets us have more than a glimpse of the creation process, so I was lucky to be with the composer John Rutter just as he finished writing his now frequently sung carol, 'Mary's Lullaby'. John described to me the moment of high exhilaration when a new piece of composition is finished and about to be performed, 'It can be rather a brief moment, because unless your action plan for several hundred people to be able to perform the work is correct, the greatest moment of elation – as the conductor raises his baton for the first note at the first rehearsal – can be followed by a rapid descent into chaos.'

John has to go off 'into the wilderness' to work, to the distraction-free surroundings of a tiny room outside his home, where he goes every morning.

'It helps to have a routine,' he said, 'but even away from the work, phrases rather mysteriously can just come into the mind.'

With such a regime, it is probably no coincidence that Rutter's *Mass of the Children*, first performed early in 2003, begins with a setting of Thomas Ken's hymn:

Awake my soul, and with the sun
thy daily stage of duty run

shake off dull sloth, and joyful rise
to pay thy morning sacrifice.

So let us now praise the men and women who make the marks on blank pieces of paper that change the world.

In 1962, two mighty acts of creation came together to influence the faith of my generation. The Cathedral Church of St Michael and All Angels in Coventry was consecrated, answering the prayers of the city, since the night the beautiful old cathedral was destroyed by bombs in November 1940, that a new building would rise from the ashes. And to mark the consecration of the new cathedral, a symbol of reconciliation and resurrection, Benjamin Britten's *War Requiem* had its first performance.

Although I only once saw Benjamin Britten at work in rehearsal, I spent many hours in the late 1970s watching John Rutter working with the Clare College Cambridge Choir, when we made two special editions of *Songs of Praise* together. Like Britten, John wins both devotion and patience from singers and instrumentalists as he helps them perfect their performance of his compositions.

Britten's *War Requiem* was a vision on a grand scale, written for a big, reverberant acoustic. As in the requiems of Verdi and Berlioz, the great hymn evoking the day of judgment, *Dies Irae*, was scored for brass playing at its most loud and terrifying, but Britten also required the distant voices of boy trebles, a choir of angels. It must have been an incredible experience for anyone lucky enough to be at the festival premiere, which celebrated the cathedral's consecration in May 1962.

A year later, the first recording was made, and in the angelic choir were two young altos, John Rutter and his friend John Taverner. The two future composers were both in the choir of Highgate School and had a unique opportunity to learn directly from Britten, who conducted the London recording himself.

'His eyes seemed to be everywhere,' remembers John Rutter. 'He was easy to work with, but you wouldn't mess him about. He didn't talk about the meaning of the work because he expected us to get that from performing it… Britten had a very precise idea of what he wanted; we in turn would have laid down our lives for him.'

Both Britten, the composer, and Basil Spence, the architect, had to live through the long and painful process from blank manuscript paper and empty drawing board to final creation at Coventry. At first, even when the work was finished, both cathedral and requiem received more brickbats and insults than praise. Yet more than anything else ever has, it was this building and this music that convinced me that the risen Jesus was close to me.

Basil Spence said he had his first inspiration in Normandy, in June 1944, just after D-Day. Dug in for the night, he was thinking about the battle he had just witnessed, as allied tanks blasted two Norman churches to winkle out German snipers in the towers, and realized then that one day he wanted to build a cathedral. In 1950, he entered – and won – the competition for 'A new cathedral in Coventry', introduced with the bishop's challenge: 'The cathedral is to speak to us and to generations to come of the Majesty, the Eternity and the Glory of God. God, therefore, direct you.'

Benjamin Britten, an avowed pacifist, was in the U.S.A. when the old Coventry cathedral was bombed. Horrified by fascism, he returned to Britain during the war, but when he was commissioned to write the *War Requiem*, it was to the poetry and music of the First World War that he turned for inspiration. As the casualties mounted in those dark days, the healing power of music had an important part to play. In one week, in the spring of 1916, Elgar's *Dream of Gerontius* was performed every day to raise funds for the Red Cross. New compositions all had a bleaker tone, described by the writer William Plomer as seeming 'to say goodbye to the vanishing peacefulness of the country and to the freshness and innocence of young men'.

In the worst days of the 'Great' War, Albert Laurie, priest of Old St Paul's Scottish Episcopal Church in Edinburgh, volunteered for chaplaincy duties. He continued to write items for his parish magazine from the front, and in 1916 reported that the heaviest enemy shelling had come on Good Friday during the three hours when his congregation at home was in church meditating on the death of Christ. And he described a great crucifix left still standing among the ruins of a French village. 'I saw as I passed in the growing dawn that the swallows were building under the crucified feet, regardless of shells and rifle bullets. Perhaps, I thought, we too are building Jerusalem by this very energy of destruction.'

The sight of a crucifix surviving through the desolation may have been quite common, for the same scene was described in a poem by Wilfred Owen, who was killed just days before the Armistice. *At a Calvary Near the Ancre* begins:

One ever hangs where shelled roads part.
In this war He too lost a limb,
But His disciples hide apart;
And now the Soldiers bear with Him.

and ends:

But they who love the greater love
Lay down their life; they do not hate.

Wilfred Owen very well fits Britten's own description of the artist who has 'an extra sensitivity – a skin less… and the great ones have an uncomfortable habit of being right about many things long before their time…' Writing to his mother just before he died, Owen ended his letter, 'If I do not read hymns, it is no bad sign. I have heard the cadences of harps not audible to Sankey, but which were strung by God; and played by mysteries to Him, and I was permitted to hear them.'

Benjamin Britten based his *War Requiem* on Wilfred Owen's poetry, and included the poem about the crucifix just prior to the moment where the Chorus sings the Agnus Dei: 'O Lamb of God, that takest away the sins of the world, have mercy on us.'

When I joined the queue to visit Coventry cathedral for the first time in 1963, I had listened and re-listened to my own poor tape recording made off a transistor radio of the *War Requiem*. Although it was long before the days of the Walkman or personal CD player, I felt I could hear the sound ringing in my ears as the great queue of visitors slowly edged forward to the door. At first we made such slow progress that it looked as if I would miss the last train back to London, but finally the pace quickened and, after a startled pause on the threshold of such a dramatic interior, we all filed around the edges.

Dispelling childhood memories of old hassocks and beeswax polish, there was a smell of something fresh and new. Everything – carvings, glass, choir stalls – was original and modern. However, because of the way we were herded, it was very hard to see the other great, controversial creation inside the new cathedral: Graham Sutherland's gigantic tapestry depicting 'Christ in Glory'. We passed almost underneath it and were then confined to the side aisle on our way back under the Paradise Lost window to the exit.

Outside again, I tried to make out the detail of the largest tapestry in the world, but the glass west wall was full of reflections of the sun. There was nothing for it. I would have to go round again, and commit an act of civil disobedience by clambering over the ropes closing off the nave. Fortunately, the queue was a little shorter this time and, being only mildly rebellious by nature, my pulse rate rose as I checked that the stewards were not looking before I leapt over the rope and into the empty nave.

Graham Sutherland had surmounted massive difficulties with the weaving as well as with critics, since he sketched out his first designs with all the dread and fear of beginning alone with an empty page.

The cathedral authorities had stipulated in their specification for the designer: 'The congregation will have no choice but to see it all the time by night as well as by day.' They added that the tapestry 'must present the timeless truths of the Christian faith which are the same for all generations'.

From the moment that I found myself in front of the tapestry, that is exactly what I felt I was being shown. Timeless truth.

The tapestry is almost 75 feet high. A team of weavers worked for two years to complete it, and Sutherland had not been able to see it hanging upright until it was placed in the cathedral a few days before the consecration. It was an act of faith as large as the tapestry itself, for the artist knew that there could be no possibility of making adjustments. It would be right or wrong.

Sutherland broke the normal silence of artists by being willing to talk about how he designed the figure of Christ in glory. The head, with eyes that seem to look intently at each person who stands before it, was less of a problem than the feet. In the end, he had to use a mirror to study his own feet before he could get it right.

When I go back now, my eyes are still first drawn to the huge, very human toes of Christ, which was what moved me first on that day when I stood in the nave and saw the tapestry clearly. Even to the sort of Christian who wants to know the precise moment and manner of being 'born again', I can honestly say that I was 'converted' one afternoon in 1963, by a building, a piece of music and a tapestry. While the tabloid press was decrying the end of the good old days of the C of E and music with recognizable tunes, I stood in my shoes and felt that I understood for the first time what the women had experienced when they went to the tomb on the first Easter morning.

Awake my soul, and with the sun
thy daily stage of duty run;
shake off dull sloth, and joyful rise
to pay thy morning sacrifice.

Redeem thy mis-spent time that's past,
live this day as if 'twere thy last:
improve thy talent with due care;
for the great Day thyself prepare.

Let all thy converse be sincere,
thy conscience as the noon-day clear;
think how all-seeing God thy ways
and all thy secret thoughts surveys.

By influence of the light Divine
let thy own light in good works shine;
reflect all heaven's propitious ways
in ardent love and cheerful praise.

Praise God, from whom all blessings flow,
praise him, all creatures here below,
praise him above, ye heavenly host,
praise Father, Son, and Holy Ghost.
Amen.

BISHOP THOMAS KEN (1637–1711)

A Working Majority

● ● ● ● ● ● ● ● ● ● ● ● ● ●

19 JUNE

In the wee small hours of these short summer nights, I can write like Shakespeare. I am not able to communicate this immediately, since neither pen nor paper is within reach, but I lie in bed, restlessly revolving, as a wonderful paragraph of perfect phrases forms in my mind. Tomorrow will be a terrific day for writing and, for once, I will really get ahead with a chapter about the animal kingdom and the kingdom of God. This is going to be good. I fall back into dreamless sleep.

Kerbang! The noise startles me awake. Was I dreaming? Kerbang! Again, and then a familiar panting sound, like an old steam engine, explains all. Downstairs in the hall MacBean is on the move. Our old dog has decided at 3 a.m. that it is time to be up and about. I lie frozen in case a movement from me suggests to him that he might be welcome upstairs. The steam engine sounds recede into the distance: he is off to his water bowl in the back kitchen. Relief. A pause. But not for long. The engine chuffs back into the hall. Then the sound I most dread – a gentle, apologetic sneeze, repeated several times, as a prelude to an elderly dog climbing the stairs. Much enthusiastic puffing indicates some hard but determined work. Then comes a series of loud, pathetic, puppy-like squeaks from behind the child gate at the top of the stairs.

The morning after MacBean first arrived from the dogs and cats' home in Edinburgh nearly two years ago, we had to strike a deal with the old, semi-blind, semi-deaf collie cross we had invited into our home. That first night, having shut our new friend into a kitchen warm from the Aga-Rayburn, Liz and I learned the first law of MacBean: doors must never be closed. All that night we lay rigidly to attention side by side as what we had taken to be a gentle, loveable, *quiet* geriatric violently assaulted the kitchen door and scrabbled at the polished floorboards, whistling, sneezing, alternately crying like a baby and barking imperiously. Knowing that we *must* not give in – we had carefully read through our *You and Your Rescue Dog* handbook – we dared not even whisper to each other in case it was picked up downstairs as the first sign of capitulation. We imagined our newly painted door being stripped, our new wooden floorboards scraped into splinters. Four hours went by before the noise gradually subsided and we must all have fallen into an anxious half-sleep for what was left of the night.

Early the next morning we went downstairs, hardly daring to imagine what destruction we would find, to discover door and floor surprisingly more or less intact, and our new 'pet' soundly asleep on his giant beanbag, and there he remained, snoring peacefully, well into mid-morning.

On the whole, at least as far as MacBean is concerned, we have had quiet nights since then. He is left free to amble about downstairs, no doors shut, until he picks up the distant sound of *Thought for the Day* on Radio 4 beside our bed, when he knows I will soon get up and remove his gate.

But tonight, for it really still is night and long before dawn, Liz is away, I am in charge of the pets, and MacBean's sneezing is the signal that means he urgently needs to 'go out in the garden'. Nothing for it, I have to get up for some crisis management.

He doesn't do it when there are two of us – only when one of us is away – and the prime suspect is his colleague Toby. Toby is a small, perfectly formed, very fine example of a pedigree Burmese red kitten who sleeps in our room because he is small and slim enough to pass through the stair-top child gate. If he wakes up in the night and fancies some fun, especially when he knows that he and MacBean have a working majority, he will run downstairs to find the old dog asleep at his post in the hall, guarding the front door, and wake him up by jumping on him. MacBean, being old, always then needs 'to go'.

Now Toby waits in the darkness to grab my toes as I wobble wearily towards the stairs. So here I am, in the middle of the night, one mere human trying to cope with the needs of two representatives of the animal kingdom which I have been planning to write deathless prose about later in the day. I tell them firmly that MacBean can go out, but Toby must not.

Halfway up the stairs MacBean checks that I really am going to deal with his problem and then begins to slither and bump his stiff old legs back down. Toby has a final grab at my pyjamas and then sails ahead of both of us, leaping over MacBean before he reaches the bottom step.

At the back door MacBean's tail wags furiously as I struggle with the locks. Then I have to pick up Toby, who seems to have developed eight wriggling legs, and hold on tight with one hand as I open the door with the other. MacBean bounces off into the garden barking furiously and triggering the security light, although in these summer months in Scotland the nearest we get to darkness is a dim twilight between midnight and 3 a.m. Toby is still determinedly struggling to join MacBean in the garden. I must not give in. Supposing he got out and got onto the road and was run over – what could I say to Liz? I shut the door firmly and put him down.

Now comes a time of waiting. Toby and I peer out through the glass door, and the security light goes out. Toby climbs to the top of the curtains to see if he can find an exit at the top, and then yells for the emergency services. (It's a Burmese thing.) I climb onto a chair and haul him back down from the ceiling. While waiting for MacBean to complete what he has to do in the garden, I stand in my pyjamas and begin to doubt whether my opening paragraph about God and the animal kingdom is going to make any sense after all, even if I can remember it in the light of day. I decide to write a few notes at the kitchen table.

Toby sits in front of me, on top of my writing pad, butting my pen and purring loudly. I give up attempts to write and stare back at him, meditating on what he and the rest of the animal kingdom have to teach us about another kingdom. (I remember filming an interview with Ursula Vaughan Williams, widow of Ralph Vaughan Williams, one of England's great composers. She was talking about her husband for the television arts programme *Omnibus*, and in a moment between filming, she showed me a piece of unfinished manuscript. It made me laugh because it was the great man's last work – and it was indelibly imprinted by the muddy paw prints of his beloved cat.)

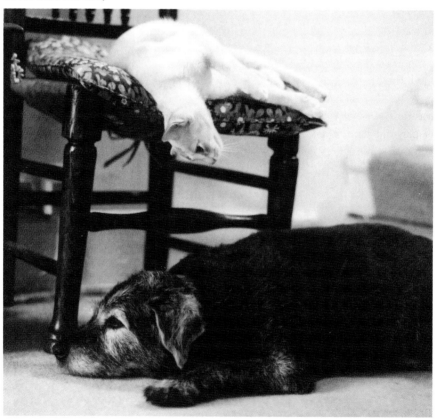

The easy option would be to prepare a plate of fish for Toby. If I am lucky, MacBean will have returned before Toby has finished his early breakfast and the door can be safely opened. The security light comes on again, and a few minutes later I can see a dark shape and eyes looking hopefully through the French windows. MacBean does not come right up to the door, but stands a little back, from where, after a moment or two of silent thought, he can make a sharp insistent bark bounce and echo off two walls, penetrating even the loudest verses of 'All creatures of our God and King' on *Songs of Praise*.

MacBean comes cautiously back in through the door, probably remembering the terrible trouble he got into soon after Toby had first arrived. Toby, coming in from the garden behind him had chosen to race gaily in under MacBean's lumbering stomach just as he was crossing the threshold. In what was either a murderous attack or an act of confused panic, the big old dog dropped on the little kitten, grabbed him in his teeth and began to shake him like a rat. We made it very clear to MacBean that if he valued his life, this behaviour was never, *ever* to be repeated. Now he confines his natural hostility to a display of silently bared teeth whenever Toby hurtles by, and it is only all the other cats that get chased out of the garden. Toby appears to think this is an act of comradeship, and constantly tries to ingratiate himself with MacBean, but it is only in my head that they are working together as a team. MacBean does not like cats at all. Never has. Never will.

Long after morning comes, I wake again to find that we have slept through *Thought for the Day* and it will be time for the *Daily Service* if I don't look sharp. I go downstairs to find MacBean and Toby sleeping peacefully in the hall, just inches apart.

I am not ready for my day's stint of writing before people are beginning to queue up at the café across the road to collect their lunchtime snacks of home-made soup and a roll. MacBean has but a light lunch, and not until after his first walk. 'Going in the garden' does not count, and the back door is for emergencies only. The wide world is only reached through the front door. By late morning he is ready and available, crossing backwards and forwards in front of me as I complete my final chores before finally getting down to write that chapter. But for now item number one is MacBean's preprandial walk. As his lead is attached he bounces up and down in excitement at the prospect of half and hour's inspection of the streets of Pathhead.

In fact this exciting itinerary so firmly set by the dog is totally predictable and, for his owners, unutterably boring. We have to go down the road in the direction of the nearby housing estate, including the circuit of a deserted children's swing park and an empty football field. All around our home are wonderful woodland walks and country lanes – but MacBean won't budge an inch if we try and entice him into the real countryside. Even on his invariable chosen route there are long views of the Moorfoot Hills and the distant Pentlands, but MacBean never gives them a glance. Head down, he sniffs his way very slowly round his familiar footpath. Sometimes I am stopped in my tracks as he drags me back to re-examine a small wooden post or the interior of a decaying bush. Nothing is ever missed and each examination is concluded with the briefest salute of his back leg. Liz says he's just dealing with his e-mails, which is now making me worry about the incoming messages on our own computer that I know will be enquiring about the progress of my writing.

For Macbean the closest thing to heaven is to come upon a trail of half-eaten burgers, fish and chips or squashed sandwiches discarded by late-night revellers. These are swallowed whole without further ado – while carefully prepared nutritious meals at home are always cautiously sniffed before being delicately nibbled at, carefully separating out anything he doesn't particularly like. On a walk he will sometimes lie down and decline to move another step in any direction. If we call his bluff and set off home without him, he calls ours, waiting until we have turned the corner and then making for the nearest open back door he has spotted, and any food bowl left down for a neighbour's pets. His deafness becomes very marked at these times, and as we have often shouted ourselves completely hoarse, the whole village has got to know the name of our dog.

Now it is night-time again, dog leads and unfinished chapters forgotten as MacBean and I amble peacefully around the old course together for the last walk of the day. Neighbourhood cats congregated under parked cars keep a watchful eye on us, but they all know that MacBean is short-sighted and preoccupied with his own business, and that outside his own garden they will rarely be noticed.

Tonight is close to midsummer, warm, still and windless. It is very quiet and I can hear MacBean's familiar panting interrupted by formidable snuffling sounds as he goes about his forensic duties. We pause in a new place, and I realize that there is a little hedgehog right under our feet, motionless, with prickles fully extended. MacBean gives a cautious sniff, and then reverts to plan.

All is peaceful, until the working majority once again goes into action. Suddenly, a little too far from the security of the garden, Toby joins us, joyfully ambushing MacBean, and then charging off before I can grab him. When Liz is at home I carry my mobile telephone to alert her when this happens, and she comes down to open the back gate, bringing a torch because so far Toby has not been able to resist chasing the beam of light until he has been guided safely back indoors. But tonight I am alone, with no torch, and Toby and MacBean both clearly know it is game on.

While MacBean, with a definite grin on his face, enjoys an extended meal of medicinal couch grass outside the back gate, eating one blade at a time, I plunge around the neighbours' gardens in pursuit of one small, high-speed, apricot-coloured cat. When I do eventually catch him, I get the feeling it is only because he feels sorry for me and has decided to give me the illusion that I can win. We return home, both jubilant, Toby grasped in my arms, and MacBean wagging his tail cheerfully before slumping straight down to his bed in the hall with a happy sigh. Toby retires to the airing cupboard and the house falls silent.

I realize that I have hung about a lot with MacBean since he came to live with us. Sometimes I have felt trapped in a sort of dog-walking groundhog's day, but at other times I have stopped and stared in the warm sunshine that has marked the last two summers in Midlothian ever since MacBean arrived. The dog has been happy; and on late summer evenings, with uncountable stars in the huge skies and a rising moon and a sun that scarcely sets, so have I.

Now before I go to bed, I really must write my chapter about the animal kingdom and the kingdom of God... If only I really could write like Shakespeare.

Bottom (awaking): I have had a most rare vision. I have had a dream, past the wit of man to say what dream it was: man is but an ass, if he go about to expound this dream. Methought I was, and methought I had, – but man is but a patcht fool, if he will offer to say what methought I had. The eye of man hath not heard, the ear of man hath not seen, man's hand is not able to taste, his tongue to conceive, nor his heart to report, what my dream was. I will get Peter Quince to write a ballet of this dream: it shall be called Bottom's Dream, because it hath no bottom; and I will sing it in the latter end of a play before the duke; peradventure, to make it the more gracious, I shall sing it at her death. (Exit.)

A MIDSUMMER NIGHT'S DREAM BY W. SHAKESPEARE (1564–1616)

Company

SUMMER

Lord Jesus Christ,
In whose company we find strength when we are weak
Light when we doubt and love when we are lonely,
Draw us to yourself tonight
And to others in the morning.
Amen.

THE *COMPANY* PRAYER

The BBC's *Epilogue* was far more varied and original than most people now remember it, but *Company*, on ITV, completely broke the mould of the television armchair pulpit. Small groups of people would sit around a kitchen table holding a late-night conversation about what they believed in, rooted not in theology but in their personal experiences of life. During the

1980s, *Company* was shown every night of the week to a growing audience on TVS, the Independent television programme maker for the South and South-East of England.

As so often with television success stories, there are differing claims as to who really invented the idea. Angus Wright, a distinguished producer who (in my view) worked in heaven, making the TV series based on the Reverend Wilbert Awdry's stories of *Thomas the Tank Engine*, was certainly in at the beginning. It was Angus who spotted the talent, not in the vestry but in the corridor outside his office, of Jo, one of the cleaners, when he realized she had a story to tell that would captivate viewers. Jo became one of the founding members of *Company*, a team of two dozen people from all walks of life who took turns, in twos, threes and fours, to sit around the kitchen table in the TVS news studio and talk to each other.

THE COMPANY TEAM WITH FRANCES TULLOCH

The audience grew quickly as viewers got to know and even to feel part of the *Company* 'family', and as time went by the team would occasionally meet together in a London church to celebrate the series with members of the audience. The *Company* family included Adrian Plass, the poet, and his wife, Bridget, Peter Timms, a Methodist minister committed to prison reform, Anne Marie Stuart, a Roman Catholic nun (now an Anglican priest), and Peter Elvy, who has become vicar of one of London's most fashionable parishes, Chelsea Old Church. *Company* was not exclusively Christian, with the late Rabbi Hugo Gryn and Rabbi David Soetendorp and his wife Ruth often taking part.

When I went to work at TVS, I came to know *Company* through a most remarkable woman, Frances Tulloch, who was, I discovered, like a mother hen to the *Company* family. Every Monday evening, four or five members of the team would assemble in a cottage deep in the countryside where they would work all evening and stay the night. Frances would ply them with tea and cakes then, beginning with Bible study, themes for a week's programming were teased out, with everyone vying for their own insights to be included. I discovered that by 1986, with hundreds of conversations already under their belts, the teams had bonded and they all knew each other well enough to fall out, oblivious of the TV cameras. They were equally adept at making newcomers welcome, as I learnt when the late Bishop Trevor Huddleston joined them, although he did seem a bit astonished when, after supper, he was expected like everyone else to get down to another *Company* tradition, team washing-up and making up of beds for the night.

The next morning, as on every Tuesday, the *Company* team for that week would go to the studio to record seven unscripted five-minute conversations, all inspired by and retaining the late-night atmosphere of discussions held well into the small hours of the night before. That they always somehow made points that communicated to a wide audience owed much to Frances's boundless enthusiasm and encyclopedic knowledge. She propelled her contributors on, by turns cajoling and caring for them. Any attempt at posturing or a lapse into pomposity was rewarded with gales of laughter and a 'Darling, that was quite dreadful, do it all again!' And they always did. Which was fortunate, since *Company* must have been one of the lowest budget programmes in TV history and editing was completely out of the question. Each programme had to fit precisely into the given time slot, which could vary considerably.

But by the end of the decade, 'late night' on *Company* started to become 'middle of the night' as ITV's night-time output developed. It was time to move on.

Quite early on in the life of *Company*, one whole week of programmes was devoted to one person's story as he faced his own death from an inoperable cancer. That person was the evangelist, Canon David Watson, who had so rejuvenated St Michael le Belfrey, the little church in the shadow of York Minster. For that week's programmes he joined Adrian and Bridget Plass and Bishop George Reindorp first in the cottage, and then at the *Company* kitchen table, sitting in his shirt sleeves and drinking coffee as he talked. He spoke openly to them about the first shock of the diagnosis, and then how he came to see the future in the light of the faith that he had devoted his life to sharing with others.

'I've always preached how wonderful heaven is going to be,' he told Bridget and Adrian, 'so if this is so, I've been wondering why I've been in such a panic! Now, how do I get theoretically to wanting to be in heaven – when practically I want to stay here on earth? People say death is the old family servant who opens the door to welcome the family home; it is just an open door. I've often said this to other people, but now I've had to say it to myself.'

Later that week, David Watson explained what had helped him most. 'I've had to learn to be totally at the receiving end of everyone else's skill and love. A Christian doctor said to me "Your best treatment is faith." But knowing that others are praying for me has been terrific. I've been kept buoyed up by unbelievably encouraging letters and calls. I have felt God's love, the God who has actually lived here on earth.'

Towards the end of the week, talking about his state of remission, David faced the hardest question: 'Am I healed? I don't know. But to others like me who are watching, I must say that reading the Psalms is incredibly helpful. A restful assurance comes that I simply cannot explain.'

Twenty years after she produced that week of programmes with David Watson, a week that generated an enormous response from the audience, Frances Tulloch was herself facing death. Listening to a radio programme that she made with her friend Olave Snelling of Premier Christian Radio just a week before she died in June 2003, I discovered that Frances once almost became a biochemist, researching a cure for cancer. She had been diverted by the world of politics and then the world of television, which had fitted the side of her personality that liked fixing up programmes at breakneck speed and developing new and risky formats. In all her different journeys and careers, however, she had never been diverted from her faith in God.

In her final broadcast, Frances prayed with Olave:

Lord, You are the God of all mercies.
We thank you for your goodness to us.
Thank you for the uncertainties,
The time when we really know your presence.

And I was reminded again of *Company*'s week with David Watson, as Frances read from a favourite psalm:

Happy those whose refuge is in you,
whose hearts are set on the pilgrim ways!
As they pass through the waterless valley
the Lord fills it with springs,
and the early rain covers it with pools.
So they pass on from outer wall to inner,
and the God of gods shows himself in Zion.
PSALM 84:5–7

Making Ministers

29 JUNE

O for a thousand tongues to sing
my great Redeemer's praise,
the glories of my God and King,
the triumphs of his grace!

CHARLES WESLEY (1707–88)

The Penrhyn quarries in north Wales once employed 3,000 men, and tourists came from all over the world to view their dangerous work, gouging slate out of a mountain. In the shadow of the quarry, at the height of its fame, men built Shiloh Chapel in Tregarth in the countryside behind the cathedral city of Bangor, where Aled Jones grew up. In Tregarth the quarrymen sang hymns in Welsh to the stern God who offered the only redemption from a cruel way of life. Now only a handful of people work in the slate quarries and an even smaller team of supporters keep the chapel intact.

On 29 June 2003, the building woke up from its slumbers as Methodists from all over the world filled every seat to witness the ordination of six men and six women as ministers. Travelling from the annual conference meeting in nearby Llandudno, they perpetuated a custom going back to the time of John and Charles Wesley that new ministers are ordained on the Sunday evening on which the conference meets.

In the seaside conference hall, a candle was lit for each of them and carried up to Shiloh Chapel where, in the presence of friends and family, each candidate had hands laid on them. Then the whole congregation shared in the communion service. For one evening Shiloh had become the centre of a

worldwide church, dramatically symbolized by the reading of the Bible by the Revd Ame Tugaue in his first language, Fijian.

As the chapel once again became a tranquil backwater, 12 new ministers set off for a life of service throughout the world, and perhaps they may never meet again. After each candidate had received the bread and the wine, the President of the Conference, the Revd Neil Richardson prayed, 'Go in peace, for Christ goes with you.'

Iesu! Yr enw a ddifa'n braw,　　　　*Jesus – the name that charms our fears,*
ffy'n gofid rhag ei wedd;　　　　　*that bids our sorrows cease;*
yn bersain at bechadur daw,　　　*'tis music in the sinner's ears,*
mae'n fywyd, iechyd, hedd.　　　　*'tis life, and health, and peace.*
　　　　　　　　　　　　　　　　CHARLES WESLEY (1707–88)

Stagger in the Stump

8 JULY

There was a Sunday evening in early 1977 when I was washing up after supper and for company had switched on the radio for *Sunday Half Hour*. I think it occurred to me then for the first time, how well a hymn tune can surprise you away from gloomy introspection. Hymn words, too, can stop you in your tracks and unlock distant memories, or even catch the imagination for something that could happen in the future. I am probably very peculiar – and my wife will tell you I am – but occasionally, listening to a huge congregation singing on a Sunday evening on the radio or television, this normally quiet, rather mixed-up low Presbyterian, high Anglo-Catholic, finds himself getting close to dancing a jig.

Sunday Half Hour on that Sunday had already begun, but as soon as I heard one particular hymn, I wanted more than anything else in the world to be there with that congregation, and for the singing to go on for ever. The sound overwhelmed me; it was as though it was heralding nothing less than Christ's return to earth, and from the way my heart was pounding as I listened, I felt as though I was there for the event. And even as I juggled the plates in the sink and began to gyrate around the kitchen, the singing of 'Mine eyes have seen the glory of the coming of the Lord' to the tune 'John Brown's Body' was bringing back a flood of other memories from my youth.

As the singing came to an end and I waited for a radio voice to tell us where we were, I realized that the sound had triggered a more than twenty-year-old memory of watching President John F. Kennedy's memorial service broadcast from St Paul's Cathedral. Shortly after my mother and father rather reluctantly joined Britain's TV-owning households in 1963, this service was shown 'live' on the BBC. On what seemed a catastrophically sad day – I had had naïve, youthful hopes that world peace would be brought about by one charismatic politician – I made a sound tape recording of the service. When they sang 'Mine eyes have seen the glory', I think that was the first time that I understood how the microphone could transport the thrilling sound from a large space of a huge congregation singing a big hymn into a small living room. I played and replayed my tape to dispel my gloom all that year, much to the irritation of my father who liked to listen to the birds from indoors. He was glad when the tape wore out.

And a year or two after that, I'm pretty sure, 'Mine eyes have seen the glory' was sung again in St Paul's, for the funeral of Sir Winston Churchill in 1965. I did remember that a little later still I was actually in the great cathedral myself, high up in the dome above the famous whispering gallery with a tape recorder. My legitimate BBC business did not involve the congregation far below, and we had been told to be unobtrusive until a memorial service was over. To my amazement, as I tested my microphone, sitting high above the organ pipes, the triumphant sound of the tune 'John Brown's Body' once more engulfed me. I will never know what words everyone was singing down below because my untransmittable but still cherished tape is as ill-balanced as it could be, with the growling 32-foot wood stops of the organ duelling with the sparkling trumpet stops. But I truly thought this was the sound of graves bursting open, even if the singing of the faithful resurrected was completely inaudible on my recording.

In 1977, all these reawakened subconscious memories must have fuelled an ambition before that hymn ended, to go as quickly as I could to wherever the singers were, and to persuade them to make what I was sure would be the *Songs of Praise* of all time. I had begun my journey to the Lincolnshire market town and port of Boston, and to a 'stagger in the Stump'.

'This is Dutch England,' wrote J.B. Priestley in *English Journey*. 'They do not call this district "Holland" for nothing… For here the country is flat; you have seen nothing raised more than 20 or 30 feet from the ground for miles and miles; and then suddenly this tower shoots up to nearly 300 feet. Your heart goes out to those old Bostonians who, weary of the Lincolnshire levels and the flat ocean, made up their minds to build and build into the blue. If God could not give them height, they would give it to Him.'

Priestley was describing his first sight of the Boston Stump, the medieval tower from which, as he put it, a 'grand old church sprouts'. As I made my way there, my own first glimpse was from near Grantham, through roadside trees far away across miles of flat fields to the east. I had already heard that birthdays and wedding anniversaries could be celebrated by paying for the floodlighting to be switched on. It looked as though the whole of Lincolnshire must celebrate red-letter days in Boston.

Lincoln is a huge county, so huge that one former archbishop of Canterbury, the late Michael Ramsey, thought that the diocese was of an unmanageable size and should be split in two. The archbishop loved Boston, and he once teased an aspiring young ordinand who hoped to train at Lincoln Theological College by suggesting, 'One day you can be bishop of Lincoln, and I shall be bishop of Boston, and it will be very good.'

When I arrived in Boston, I realized that I would need all my television wits about me to convey on the screen anything like the dramatic effect the Stump creates in reality. It is as exciting to look at on the outside as the sound I had heard broadcast coming from inside, but John Logie Baird did not make televisions to record high, slender towers, and viewers' TV sets would need to be turned on their sides to get the full impact of this tremendous edifice built over years by at least four architects.

There are two ways of seeing it: it either catches you unawares as you peer down the narrow streets of the old market town, or it suddenly materializes from miles away, far across the flat Lincolnshire landscape. There is a third way – from ships out in the North Sea, for which the many tall East Anglian church spires act as lighthouses – but that was out of the question on my programme budget. I wanted to show it by day, and also in its full glory, floodlit at night, which could only be captured by running a film camera at slow speed and using a special wide-angle lens, which in those days was hard to obtain.

With the sound of *Sunday Half Hour* still in my head, I began to learn one of the hard lessons for a *Songs of Praise* director: stunningly beautiful churches offer so many alternative images that the plot that really matters can all too easily be lost. If you spend too much time and effort setting up beautiful shots, the community that have gathered together to sing their hymns, the whole heart of the programme after all, can grow tired and bored and feel neglected.

There was so much potential for the TV cameras in the Stump, but how much could we afford to light the huge building – always the most expensive part of an outside broadcast – and even once the lights were in place, how much of the extremely lofty interior would the cameras be able to see if they were mainly looking at people singing? Where could the microphones be placed without spoiling all the pictures if we were to hear the effect of the singers massed in the nave? Almost certainly, the choirs for *Sunday Half Hour* had been grouped around huge metal microphone stands and in practice a relatively small number of choristers could have sounded like a multitude when recorded. Radio is good at illusions, but for TV we had to fill the enormous church to satisfy the camera lens, so would that mean getting the whole diocese to travel to what J.B. Priestley called 'this odd corner' of England?

I was hoping against hope that someone in Boston would choose 'John Brown's Body'. Ray Short, Methodist minister and *Songs of Praise*'s editor at the time, was rather strict, insisting that it was only the community's own choices that were broadcast, not hymns his directors or producers fancied. (He had already bombed out my earlier attempts to include a hymn that

had caught my imagination as a child in St George's, Beckenham. The Victorian processional hymn 'Trumpet of God, sound high' to the tune 'Rangoon' was a step too far for Ray, with its second line "till the hearts of the heathen shake'.) But in Boston, he did agree to my proposal that the choir should enter up the wide nave in procession singing whatever first hymn was chosen.

Entirely without prompting, the researcher, Liz (now my wife), returned from a look around Boston and recommended Mike Haynes, Scout leader of the 5th Boston St Botolph Troop as one of the interviewees. Mike wanted to show how the Scout movement not only helped individuals to be self-sufficient but also to develop into citizens proud to be part of their community. To illustrate this, he had suggested 'Mine eyes have seen the glory', a hymn that everyone enjoyed singing at the Scouts Annual Festival in the Stump. I was in luck.

A tatty yellow script dug out of the garage this year is all that remains of the proceedings from that night which TV directors call the 'stagger', the camera rehearsal for the benefit of the director and technicians, which singers have to endure the night before the hymns are recorded. In Boston it was scheduled for Thursday 7 July, a hot, sticky night when, with the great doors of the Stump wide open, the camera crew and I started to test out the 111 different shots with which I planned to cover no less than nine hymns and a mini-drama. This latter was another overambitious idea of mine, never before attempted on *Songs of Praise*, but on the staff of Boston Stump at the time was an equally enthusiastic priest, Kenneth Stevenson, now the bishop of Portsmouth. His mini-drama imagined a stark encounter between Saints Francis and Clare and the devil trying slyly to tempt them both from the way of sanctity.

We were in for a long, hard 'stagger'. Scrawled over my old script are the notes I made as we battled through each shot. When it came to 'Mine eyes have seen the glory', Julia Ward Howe's words and William Steffe's tune suggest a community on the march and ideally this is done by moving cameras past the ranks of singers. However, all that the Stump's old, worn floor would allow the cameras to do was a lurching wobble. The 'stagger' ground to a halt and I had to think again. I tried instead contrasting very close shots of individuals and huge wide shots looking in all directions at the church, since this seemed to match the mood of the time and the message of the words.

Whenever I watch *Songs of Praise*, I still look to see if today's directors have the same ideas. Try it out yourself when you next watch, by imagining how you would use four or five cameras in different positions in the church to communicate the meaning of a hymn and what sort of shots should come up. For instance, some hymns are intensely personal and suggest close-ups, while others show faith strengthened by others, so you film the singers in groups, and perhaps slowly pull out to show they all belong to an even larger choir.

My notes from the Boston stagger also show that I had made no allowance for the big camera cables which had to run the full length of the nave and, not for the first time, I had left too little room for the cameras to hide from each other. It was quite a mess. (Fortunately, the stern Ray Short was not present.) But Church of England bishops either have short memories or very forgiving natures. Kenneth Stevenson has taken part in *Songs of Praise* several times since the night we rehearsed his play in Boston. Repeatedly, I had to ask the two young children, Paul (Francis) and Sandra (Clare) to freeze position in mid-flight while we worked out why the cameras were looking at each other and not at the actors. In those days, the camera taking a close-up needed to be much closer than today. Corrine Ransom playing the devil in a bright red suit had an even more impossible task, hiding behind the old chancel rail and then leaping dramatically onto a pillar. Our 'stagger' must have felt more like the preparations for Olympic athletics.

It was a tribute to the patience and skill of the young actors, to a huge, patient and tuneful choir under conductor David Wright, to a much-loved priest, the late Canon Trevor Collins, and the BBC team headed by another Trevor, the senior cameraman, that everything came together perfectly on the summer night of Friday 8 July.

The tracery in the west window etched the sunset at the end of a beautiful summer day as the choir, led by a processional cross and candles, moved up the centre aisle singing 'All my hope on God is founded' to Herbert Howell's tune 'Michael'. As the organist, Eric Wayman, played over the tune, I was able to use a filmed shot which, up until then, many thought was impossible. Film cameraman Keith Hopper had held his camera on its back to look straight up inside the soaring Stump and gently turned it on its axis, so that as the image revolved showing the whole tower rising overhead I could slowly mix to the processional cross on the word 'God'.

Thankfully everyone had returned for the recording, including the redoubtable Miss Barbara Brierley and Miss Lois Beaulah, two retired missionaries who had chosen John Keble's 'Blest are the pure in heart'. I still remember their wonderful resilience as they talked about their hymn 'on camera', walking together across the fens, in spite of having just driven their car through the rear wall of the garage after a brake failure. They had emerged a bit dusty but without fuss to cope with all the exotic rituals of film-making. As so often on *Songs of Praise*, their few minutes helped capture both the spirit of community and a deep personal faith in God, which makes every programme a fresh and surprising experience.

'We've chosen Keble's hymn,' said Miss Beaulah, 'because it is short and simple with only four verses. The first two verses describe the Incarnation and the kingship of Christ, and then you can use the last verses as a prayer. And the tune "Franconia" is nice for people like me who can't sing at all.'

What about Mike Haynes and his Scouts and 'Mine eyes have seen the glory'? They were all in the Stump filling the chancel. The singing was terrific and lifted the roof. It was everything I had hoped for. The 'Stump' and the Boston community made a programme whose sights and smells still draw me back to visit the town. But the restless world of TV and the restless world of the director had sent me off with a new ambition: to find a church where another community could convey again my new-found enthusiasm, which had emerged in the 'stagger', for 'Blest are the pure in heart.'

The Home Front

● ● ● ● ● ● ● ● ● ● ● ● ● ● ●

SUMMER

'I had a strange vision one evening that summer, of going to lean on a five-barred gate and looking across a beautiful field. Twenty miles away, above the English Channel, I heard the distant sound of battle, and as I looked I was overwhelmed by a ferocious feeling, like falling in love. This is our country. This must never be invaded. That was the message of the view.

'I've never seen that view again, because I've never been able to find the gate and the field again. I have a feeling now that it doesn't exist.'

DAPHNE CLAY, IN GOUDHURST, KENT, TALKING ABOUT HER MEMORIES
OF THE BATTLE OF BRITAIN

In the seventeenth century, the Puritan soldiers of Cromwell's army often thought they could see a battle between heaven and hell being fought in the skies above England, but in the summer of 1940 the battle in the skies became terrifyingly real as 'The Few', the fighter pilots of the RAF, although overwhelmingly outnumbered, fought on in one-to-one combat with the German Luftwaffe, diving and wheeling over the English countryside. France had fallen and Nazi troops were poised to invade Britain. Winston Churchill, the new prime minister, said in a broadcast: 'The survival of Christian civilization is at stake.'

Daphne Clay's 'vision', looking across the golden field, must have been a typical one for the people of the villages of Kent, who found themselves daily in the stalls of a terrifying theatre. The drama in the skies above their heads was a real life and death one, but they could only watch as first man took on man and the tiny Spitfires and Hurricanes tried to outwit the Messerschmitt 109s and then the waves of Heinkel and Dornier bombers intent on destroying Britain's airfields.

Songs of Praise has told many stories of the Battle of Britain over the years, but not from Goudhurst, where a programme was made in 1994. Since the village was my home, I heard the story of what happened in that summer of 1940.

The Battle of Britain began in earnest on 10 July. Down below, the village of Goudhurst, perched on top of a hill, was very vulnerable, but everyone was on the alert for the enemy. Daphne Clay, a member of the Red Cross, was at her first-aid post, ready for the fight. 'If enemy parachutists had landed in the hop gardens, they would have been in a spot of trouble,' she recalled cheerfully years later.

As the summer went on, the conflict escalated. Weapons and the victims of war fell out of the sky. In the 1980s, older residents of Goudhurst recalled

the Battle of Britain victims of what we now call 'friendly fire', when no less than five RAF Hurricane fighters collided in mid-air over the village. Women sorting the harvest of hops brought in from the fields to the comparative safety of the trees by the village pond, fainted in horror at the sight. The hop pickers from the East End of London, who regularly came down for a working holiday, found they were now in the front line.

In the air, the young RAF pilots demonstrated almost miraculous skills in combat. They had only seconds to attack before they were attacked, and the machine guns in the wings had only enough ammunition to last 12 seconds. 'All the training in the world cannot train you for real combat – and to face death,' said one survivor.

Daphne Clay had her own experience of these extraordinary young men when they came down to earth. On 16 August, an RAF pilot drifted across the village with his parachute open, but on fire. 'He survived because the wind dropped suddenly and he was brought in to us desperately ill with all his uniform charred. But he immediately demanded to use the telephone, saying, "I must ring up my wife or I will be reported dead."'

Another pilot, Flying Officer Elliott, also came in with serious burns, but fortified himself with the whisky flask concealed in his uniform, before insisting on supervising the wrapping-up of his parachute. It was his own, and had cost him £70, a fortune in the 1940s.

Richard Lenz, the first German pilot to reach the village, did not survive. His parachute did not open and he was buried in the village cemetery. Later, his remains were returned to Germany, but until then his grave had always been discreetly tended by a local woman from a family with German origins. Everyone knew, but even 60 years on, people wondered whether this was something that could be mentioned.

Even Daphne Clay's Red Cross post was in danger. On 20 August, just after lunch as the local volunteer ambulance crew returned to their garage, it was sprayed with machine gun bullets.

On 3 September 1940, the local Home Guard, based on the top of the parish church tower, logged a message: 'Four German spies reported to have landed on the coast.' It was a fine, hot day and there was an air-raid alert lasting three hours. The report was unfounded, but it must have been difficult not to feel jittery even on a day of cloudless, blue skies.

The worst day of the Battle of Britain was 15 September 1940. Miss Edna Percy, for many years the organist of nearby Kilndown Church, remembered: 'I didn't have lunch that day, because the enemy bombers came over in two huge waves like rooks. Some of them were so low, we could look down on them with their trailing aerials knocking apples off the trees.'

Near her home at 3.15 p.m., a huge Dornier bomber crashed. A member of the Home Guard went to investigate and was killed as the aircraft blew up. Although that afternoon marked the turning point in the battle, it was one of the worst days of Goudhurst's war.

Later that month, the vicar's letter in the Parish magazine gave an insight into church life that summer. He wrote, 'My dear friends, the congregation is to be congratulated on its calm. During our service, a nearby bomb caused no apparent consternation from what I could see from the pulpit – although it may have roused a few slumberers in the pews.'

In 1941, the church was severely damaged when two land mines fell on the vicarage, fortunately when no one was at home. It was a wet, foggy night and Daphne Clay had been on duty nearby. 'We heard the sad tinkling of our greenhouse going for a Burton (which unbelievably had once been used by the Home Guard for shelter). The dog's door had blown in and he was tearing around the fields.'

Next morning, the whole village was out clearing up the mess, and mercifully the Red Cross log contained only one new entry. Another dog had bitten its owner in alarm, and was duly recorded as 'dog bite due to enemy action'.

In 1990, Sir Harry Secombe visited one of the most famous RAF Fighter Stations at Biggin Hill for *Highway*. In St George's Memorial Chapel, from where the first televised service was transmitted after the war, he sang 'O God, our help in ages past'.

THE AUTHOR AND HARRY SECOMBE AT RAF BIGGINHILL

The chapel records the names of 450 people from 52 squadrons who died on active service, in the air and on the ground, in the sector that includes the sky over Kent. Perhaps, having heard the stories of Daphne Clay and her friends in Goudhurst, and the stories told to Sir Harry at Biggin Hill, I should have ignored John Wesley's alteration and reverted to Isaac Watt's original words: 'Our God, our help in ages past'. For the Battle of Britain was an almost unsurpassed team effort. Alone in the sky, the heroism of such young men, and later quite a few older sergeant pilots who came in for the final desperate battle on 15 September 1940, was unmatched, but it is clear to me that the courage and steadfastness of thousands of others below also made a difference.

One of the people on the ground was 1212094 Max Bygraves, who joined the RAF at 17 in September 1940, and carried out maintenance work on the Spitfires at RAF Hornchurch. 'We were teenagers who suddenly became men,' he told Sir Harry. 'In the barrack room, one man used to get down on his knees every night. He never asked for silence, but we were all there with him.'

If these stories describe heroics that seem beyond the reach of the rest of us, here is an unpublished poem written during the Battle of Britain by the late Chairman of the Battle of Britain Pilots' Association, Sir Christopher Foxley-Norris. He said to Sir Harry, 'We were very frightened and very ignorant and sometimes rather indignant. We knew what the fox felt when the chase was on, and so I wrote this to be a poem about the ordinary airman.'

Remember him
He was no Galahad, no knight sans peur et sans reproche.
Sans peur?
Fear was the second enemy to beat.
He was a common, unconsidered man who for a moment of eternity
Held the whole future of mankind in his two sweating palms
And did not let go.
Remember him
Not as he is portrayed, but as he was,
For to him you owe the most of what you have and love today.

SIR CHRISTOPHER FOXLEY-NORRIS (1917–2003)

Autumn:
October to December

In God's Own Field

● ● ● ● ● ● ● ● ● ● ● ● ● ●

HARVEST

Sooner or later, almost everyone has a baptism in country lore, and usually haymaking is the ceremony. It's a trap that the country springs on even the most urbane of visitors to teach them how busy life is on the sleepy-looking land.

JOHN BULL MAGAZINE, 27 AUGUST 1955

I had no doubt as a child that I would grow up to be a farmer. While my brother brought out his collection of model tanks and howitzers on Sundays, I would set up my collection of farm models, with black-and-white cows, the shepherd (who had two sheep and one lamb) and the milkmaid. The most treasured toys were the 'farm things', a model Fordson tractor and, best of all, a Massey Ferguson combine harvester. I hadn't the faintest idea about real farming, but my belief that the farmer's life was all about feeding pet animals nicely and driving massive machines for a few weeks in the summer was because this was all I could see of it, as we ventured out from the suburbs for what John Bull calls the 'baptism in country lore'.

Today, even though I live in the heart of Midlothian countryside surrounded by acres of farmland, where the harsh yellow flowers of oil seed rape are followed by golden heads of corn and barley, I am still lucky to see much of the 'farm things'. It is after dark when the huge combine harvester roars down our village street, and turns into the fields where the tall waving crops have whispered and rustled in the summer sunshine as the dog and I pass by. Cutting and harvesting by the light of huge headlamps, the operator, wearing ear defenders and sitting high up in his air-conditioned cabin, clears the largest field in a matter of hours. Next morning, the fields around us are bare and silent. Tractors hauling trailers overflowing with grain have passed our house throughout the summer night, and 'all is safely gathered in' several weeks before the autumn evening when *Songs of Praise* will celebrate the harvest on television.

As Aled Jones discovered when he met some of Devonshire's farmers for Harvest *Songs of Praise* from Exeter Cathedral in 2003, farming today can be a hard and lonely life. In the highly mechanized industry, far fewer people are needed to work on the land, and those that do have to cope not only with the unpredictable British climate, but these days with increasingly complex European Community regulations that mean that today's farmer spends more time on a computer than in the fields.

'A lot of farmers feel that they are the ones who are failing, and they need to be cheered up,' Nick Viney, organizer of the Devon Farm Groups, told Aled when he visited one of their regular barbecues. The group has no set agenda, but is a meeting place where new legislation is explained, and where the members talk about their difficulties and pray together.

'I can't understand,' said one young farmer, 'how anyone can work under the stars and in the sunshine and believe that creation is just an accident.' Not all the members are Christians but, as Nick Viney said, 'We may face all sorts of problems, but we're here together to face them.' Looking back to the disastrous outbreak of foot-and-mouth disease in 2002, when Devon was especially hard hit, Nick recalled: 'We could e-mail each other, weep on the telephone with each other, send prayers to each other and look after each other then. I think we could almost live through anything now.'

Those Devon farmers and their families and friends, gathered for their celebration barbecue after a good year in 2003, were a reminder of how once farming and rural community life were closely bound together. A hundred years ago the whole village would turn out for harvesting, and school was suspended. Gathering in a good harvest was a matter of life and death. In early nineteenth-century Devon, the fields would have become a scene of frenzied activity that only paused when all the wheat was cut and the 'Harvest Holla' was declared. Then gleaning was permitted, and mothers and children could gather up anything left behind for their own use.

Everything to do with the harvest in those days relied on hard manual work and the relationship between man and beast. In the fields, scythe and pitchfork skills were vital. The crop was threshed in barns, often by teams working rhythmically and calling aloud each move as the sheaves were turned over. The sheaves were then piled up and carried on horseback along the narrow lanes. The farmer's boy would perch on top, leading a whole string of horses and try to 'travel them soberly', as a contemporary observer wrote, back to the farmyard. The loads would be pushed over each horse's tail onto the haystack and then, to celebrate the task completed: 'The boy stands upright and trots, or perhaps gallops, back to the field; frequently, to the no small dismay or perhaps injury of peaceful travellers… A somewhat uncivilized practice.'

The idea of autumn Harvest Thanksgiving as part of the church's year was first introduced in 1843 by a country parson, the Reverend Robert Hawker, vicar of Morwenstow, a parish on the north coast of Cornwall. He was concerned for two reasons. First of all, that year, the harvest had been a failure, and the people who would suffer would be the poor of his parish. Secondly, the farm workers were up in arms because, added to the sound of horses and threshing choruses, was the clanking, hissing and puffing of the steam engine. Catalogues were enticing farmers with labour-saving pairs of steam engines, which could haul a plough across the fields, replacing teams

A HYMN FOR THE HARVEST of 1847.

(COMPOSED FOR THE THANKSGIVING-DAY.)

of workers with just two men. Armies of farm labourers, faced with the loss of their livelihoods, had banded together to resist. In July 1844, the *Illustrated London News* reported incendiarism in Essex. A barn full of wheat was destroyed and the report ended:

The crime appears to have been committed because Mr Chinery, the farmer, used a dressing-machine and is a maker of machinery.

The Revd Robert Hawker wanted both to encourage his parishioners to distribute food to the poor, and to stem the tide of revolution which he saw to be as much a threat as the new machinery to the life of the countryside.

Unlike in 1843, Britain was blessed with a rich harvest in 1844. 'Let the poor man rejoice – there will be this season no lack of the staff of life,' wrote the editor of the *Illustrated London News*, hoping that full stomachs would bring an end to the workers' revolt. And in 1847, in spite of food riots in Devonshire, the editor was still full of Victorian optimism, publishing a poem worthy of the poet McGonagall, but written by 'L', to commemorate the Meeting of the Royal Agricultural Society at Northampton:

God speed the Plough! Here in Northampton meet
The sons of Ceres: 'tis her festival;
The peasant, yeoman and the land's elite,
From cottage, homestead, and baronial hall,
Come with the pride of garden, pen and stall,
Competitors. E'en royalty will strive,
Proud of the prize which may it befall;
Though won by tenant of the humble hive,
Long may such scenes ennoble England fair;
For noble are they – bringing high and low
Into communion worthy as 'tis rare,
Making the heart of honest labour glow.
Heaven shield the enterprise of mine and rail,
And speed the plough, the loom and freedom's sail.

Unemployment remains one of the great problems for rural communities. But over 150 years later, the churches and farmers have found a new common purpose. In the Exeter Harvest *Songs of Praise*, Aled Jones was asked to compare two apples, one imported from New Zealand and the other locally grown, as Sue Errington explained the idea behind the Devon churches' 'Food for Thought' Campaign, which encourages people to choose local, organic and Fair Trade food. She said, 'It gets more quickly to the table, so it tastes better. If we are going to maintain our countryside, then we must support our local growers.'

In nearby Honiton market, Helen Barrett said that in buying 'fairly traded' food, we would be certain that a fair price had been paid to growers not just at home, but all over the world. 'It makes a difference in their lives, their children can be educated, medical needs answered and sometimes it is as simple as putting a roof over their heads.'

Those few minutes in Devon's Honiton market showed *Songs of Praise* viewers how much we all need to be more aware of our neighbours all over the world in our ordinary everyday lives. We have come a long way from the Harvest Festival days when a London church magazine offered 'Miss Minnie Moore's Missionary Marmalade' to readers, and when tins of fruit salad and baked beans were placed on the altar. Yet Harvest *Songs of Praise* from Devon revealed that there is still a long way to go before we live up to the words of this hymn, which first appeared in 1844, a year when, like 2003, the harvest was particularly plentiful:

All the world is God's own field,
fruit unto his praise to yield,
wheat and tares together sown,
unto joy or sorrow grown:
first the blade and then the ear,
then the full corn shall appear:
grant, O harvest Lord, that we
wholesome grain and pure may be.
HENRY ALFORD (1810–71)

Saints and Sinners

• • • • • • • • • • • • • •

2 NOVEMBER, ALL SOULS' DAY

O blest communion! Fellowship divine!
We feebly struggle, they in glory shine;
yet all are one in thee, for all are thine.
Alleluia!

FROM *FOR ALL THE SAINTS* BY W. WALSHAM HOW (1823–97)

The thing that has helped me remember so much about the long history of *Songs of Praise* is that my mind works in pictures. Often I will remember what someone said because I can remember exactly where they were and how they looked when they said it. And I can remember where and when hymns were sung, through remembering the image of particular 'shots' that I, or some other director, used to illustrate them. It comes back like a photograph, and I have a big collection of these stored snapshot memories related to all the years I have watched and worked on *Songs of Praise*.

So today I can download a memory of Sir Harry Secombe singing Cecil Spring Rice's hymn 'I vow to thee my country' because I can visualize him standing on the white cliffs of Dover when he sang it. He is in profile, about 50 yards away from me, leaning back slightly, a characteristic performance pose and, from where I am standing, he seems to be in the middle of a gorse bush in full flower. There is no such shot in *Highway* from Dover, but it is this incongruous image that often comes to me when I remember Sir Harry.

Actual photographs or portraits of family and friends are often disconnected from any particular event, so are less effective than the pictures in my mind at bringing back memories. They often show people smiling, but if a memory of the actual moment is to come back, it is better when the photographer has caught the subject unawares. I managed to photograph the late Dame Thora Hird and her beloved 'Scottie' at a dinner celebrating – I think – her 80th birthday. I caught her in one of her 'I'm here to tell you' moments, in full flow,

156

leaning forward, gesticulating with one hand at some unseen guest in mock challenge, as one hilarious anecdote flowed into another. Looking at Scottie's face, I can remember exactly what he was about to say: 'O Thor!' – his frequent half serious, half laughing reproachful response to his dear Thor's excesses.

On All Souls' Day, when we pray for all the people we have 'known and loved but see no more', I am particularly grateful for the pictures in my mind. As long as my brain works they will always be with me, and as the years of separation grow the happy memories are the ones that remain most vividly. I remember the saints and sinners of my own past in these pictures, and on All Soul's Day in particular I thank God for Sir Harry and Dame Thora, and for all the other people from in front of and behind the cameras, whose lives have made up the story so far of *Songs of Praise*.

The souls of the righteous are in the hand of God,
and no torment will ever touch them.
In the eyes of the foolish they seemed to have died,
and their departure was thought to be a disaster,
and their going from us to be their destruction;
but they are at peace.
For though in the sight of others they were punished,
their hope is fully of immortality.
Having been disciplined a little, they will receive great good,
because God tested them and found them worthy of himself;
like gold in the furnace he tried them,
and like a sacrificial burnt-offering he accepted them.
In the time of their visitation they will shine forth,
and will run like sparks though the stubble.
They will govern nations and rule over peoples,
and the Lord will reign over them for ever.
Those who trust in him will understand truth,
and the faithful will abide with him in love,
because grace and mercy are upon his holy ones,
and he watches over his elect.

WISDOM 3:1–9

Glory to Thee

• • • • • • • • • • • • • •

NOVEMBER

Bishop Thomas Ken is commemorated in a stained-glass window in the Anglican cathedral in Portsmouth. During final preparations for *Songs of Praise* from the cathedral, the evening sun lights up his memorial, which faces across the Solent to the Isle of Wight where he wrote this hymn. Mrs C.F. Alexander, fellow hymn writer, wrote of this hymn: 'No other is so suitable to the homely pathos and majesty of the English liturgy.'

Glory to thee, my God, this night
for all the blessings of the light;
keep me, O keep me, King of kings,
beneath thine own almighty wings.

Forgive me, Lord, for thy dear Son,
the ill that I this day have done,
that with the world, myself, and thee,
I, ere I sleep, at peace may be.

Teach me to live, that I may dread
the grave as little as my bed;
teach me to die, that so I may
rise glorious at the judgement day.

O may my soul on thee repose,
and may sweet sleep mine eyelids close –
sleep that shall me more vigorous make
to serve my God when I awake.

When in the night I sleepless lie,
my mind with heavenly thoughts supply;
let no ill dreams disturb my rest,
no powers of darkness me molest.

Praise God, from whom all blessings flow;
praise him, all creatures here below,
praise him above, ye heavenly host,
praise Father, Son, and Holy Ghost.

THOMAS KEN (1637–1711)

Portsmouth Remembers

● ● ● ● ● ● ● ● ● ● ● ● ●

At the mouth of the great natural harbour, which for centuries has been home to the ships of the Royal Navy based at Portsmouth, is a peaceful corner of the busy city, appearing to stand guard over the narrow entrance. Tourists exploring Old Portsmouth may sometimes see a ship of the Royal Navy squeeze through. Even in a city where *HMS Victory* and *HMS Warrior*, our most historic British warships, are preserved, nothing is more memorable than the sight of an aircraft carrier on active service, going to sea or returning to port, towering over the houses as it glides past, the crew lined up on the flight deck. Sometimes a band is playing, as it was early in 1982 when the Royal Navy's task force left Portsmouth for the South Atlantic watched by thousands of cheering well wishers. Many months later they sailed home and the news cameras and the crowds were there again to

HMS ARK ROYAL LEAVING PORTSMOUTH

see the boys who had gone to the Falklands return as men.

Scarcely a hundred yards from the water's edge is St Thomas's Cathedral. Inside, a gravestone is set in the floor, always strewn with fresh sprigs of rosemary, the herb for remembrance that would have been familiar to the sixteenth-century sailors whose bones are buried there. It marks a national tragedy in 1545 when, in full view of watching families and of the king himself, Henry VIII's flagship, the *Mary Rose*, capsized and vanished under the waters of the Solent and everyone on board was drowned.

When men and women from all three armed services came to Portsmouth Cathedral in 2003 for *Songs of Praise* for Remembrance, they stood in silence a few yards away from this grave and remembered not only centuries of lives sacrificed in war, but also all the victims of accidents and 'friendly fire' which

result from the continuing conflicts today. It is a sad and sobering fact that, apart from 1968, men and women in the services have died on duty every year since the end of World War II.

As the last post was sounded in Portsmouth by buglers from the Royal Marines, and the Standards were lowered, old comrades were remembered by the smartly turned-out veterans who stood to attention amongst today's service personnel.

George Baker, bearer of the Royal Army Service Corps Standard, my father's regiment, was almost the first person to arrive for the recording. He wanted to ensure that he had properly prepared for the sombre moment when the standard was first lowered and then raised at the reveille, a manoeuvre which is less easy than it looks, especially in such emotional circumstances.

Rachel Holmes, a naval officer who hardly looked old enough to have left school, had her own memories as she stood to attention in the nave of Portsmouth Cathedral that day. In March 2003, only four months after she joined the Navy, Rachel was a member of the crew of the aircraft carrier *HMS Ark Royal*, playing her part in the war with Iraq. She told Pam Rhodes, 'When you are interviewed for the Navy, you are asked: 'What do you feel about war?' since war is in the nature of our job. You don't think "Soon it might involve me," but after four months I found myself in the situation.'

While at sea, going in support of the Royal Marines landing in southern Iraq, Rachel, who plays the saxophone, joined a volunteer band. 'Sometimes there were as many as a dozen of us to play the hymns for the church service on the quarter deck each Sunday.' Another member of the band was Mark Lawrence, who played the euphonium and was a crewmember on one of *Ark Royal*'s sea king helicopters. The helicopters operated day and night in difficult flying conditions. Mark was one of seven crewmen who died on 22 March 2003 when two helicopters collided in the dark. Like the sinking of the *Mary Rose*, it was a tragic accident.

Rachel said, 'Certainly what's happened has changed my perception of war and changed my view of Remembrance Sunday. The reality is that it's happening all the time. Whether in an accident or in combat, people have died serving their country and I have a lot of admiration for that.

'We had a memorial service on the day after the accident; feelings were raw, but it was profoundly moving.' One of Mark's senior colleagues had suggested that a seat be left in the band, covered with a flag on which Mark's euphonium was laid. 'We played "Abide with me" and every verse I felt was fabulous.'

Watching the march past the Cenotaph in Whitehall on Remembrance Sunday, it is all too easy to think of war as the business of old men. The determined expression, the smart bearing and the immaculate 'eyes left' as rank after rank marches past, make haunting television pictures. But

Rachel's story has reminded us of the true image of war: the fresh, young, smiling face of Mark from the helicopter crew who died on duty in 2003, the young sailors on the *Mary Rose*, the boys and girls who die on duty in every war. For people of my generation, born in World War II, the men and women who go to war today are our grandchildren.

Now only a last handful of centenarians are left to represent the millions of young men who went into action in the First World War. Soon they too will be gone, just as the parade in Whitehall vanishes each year, leaving a sea of poppy wreaths around the Cenotaph. So every year at Remembrance-tide, we pause to remember the young who, in the words of the epitaph they used to commemorate the Battle of Kohima Ridge, ask:

'When you go home, tell them and say
For your tomorrow, we gave our today.'

'WE WILL REMEMBER THEM' PORTSMOUTH

A Hymn for Remembrance Sunday

God! As with silent hearts we bring to mind
How hate and war diminish humankind,
We pause – and seek in worship to increase
Our knowledge of the things that make for peace.

Hallow our will as humbly we recall
The lives of those who gave and give their all.
We thank you, Lord, for women, children, men
Who seek to serve in love, today as then.

Give us deep faith to comfort those who mourn,
High hope to share with all the newly born,
Strong love in our pursuit of human worth:
'lest we forget' the future of this earth.

So, Prince of Peace, disarm our trust in power,
Teach us to coax the plant of peace to flower.
May we, im-passioned by your living Word,
Remember forward to a world restored.

FRED KAAN (B. 1929)

A Prayer for Use During an Air Raid

NOVEMBER

O God, beneath the shadow of whose wings Thy saints ever dwell secure, we praise Thee for thy matchless justice and for Thine unending love. We beseech Thee to forgive us for the sins of our nation which are our sins, and for this blasphemy of war.

Hear us for those who suffer; in our country and in every other; and for our enemies, above all for those who seek our life.

And grant us grace at this present time to surrender our lives to Thy divine will, either for life or for death; for death, if by dying we can make reparation for sin and add our suffering to those of Christ for his body's sake, which is the Church; for life, if by living we may serve each other for whom Christ suffered, and help to build up in equity a world broken down by sin.

Amen

AUTHOR UNKNOWN

I wonder how many people who lived through the Blitz in the Second World War, when enemy bombers would appear in the skies every evening as darkness fell, recognize this prayer? The Reverend Hugh Graham is the present minister of the Stepney Meeting House, home for a small but thriving congregation, which also offers hospitality to all of the East End of London's multicultural community. He showed me this 'Prayer for use during an air raid', which he had discovered typed on a small, fragile piece of paper among the church's records of the terrifying days of the Blitz.

The prayer may well have been written by the Reverend Alec Miller, who was minister in Stepney between 1940 and 1942, and who later left East London to work with the Iona Community's founder, George MacLeod, in Glasgow. In those days the Stepney Meeting House was the John Knox Presbyterian church, and during the bombing in 1940, the congregation welcomed people from two other churches after their buildings were destroyed. It was their turn in 1941, when their own church was blitzed. Fortunately nobody was sheltering inside when the bombs fell.

Hear us for those who suffer; in our country and in every other; and for our enemies, above all for those who seek our life.

We know that this prayer was in regular use in the church all through those dark days. It must have taken great courage and faith to say the words and mean them.

In 1956, a new church was completed on the site, today's Meeting House. The wall facing the street was deliberately left blank by the architect. Respecting the church's tradition of wartime hospitality, he hoped that, like a walled garden, passing strangers would come inside to discover for themselves what the Meeting House had to offer to the neighbourhood. Then they would go out strengthened and find that, as the unknown writer of the prayer believed, God's unending love would be with them, however uncertain the times.

As our small group, all from different denominations, passed newspaper hoardings warning of terrorist attacks in London and walked by the blank wall of the Meeting House, we joined boisterous young men from the Bangladeshi community coming into their sports club in the church hall.

One of them, living nearby, told us he likes to hear the Sunday morning bell as he wakes up: 'When it stops, I know that it's time for my bath.'

Jesus the Lord said, I am the bread,
the bread of life for the world am I.

Jesus the Lord said, I am the door,
the way and the door for the poor am I.

Jesus the Lord said, I am the light,
the one true light of the world am I.

Jesus the Lord said, I am the shepherd,
the one good shepherd of the sheep am I.

Jesus the Lord said, I am the life,
the resurrection and the life am I.

AN URDU HYMN TRANSLATED BY C.D. MONAGHAN (1906–57) AND SUNG IN CANTERBURY
CATHEDRAL AT THE ENTHRONEMENT OF ROWAN WILLIAMS, ARCHBISHOP OF CANTERBURY

Doon the Watter

● ● ● ● ● ● ● ● ● ● ● ● ●

30 NOVEMBER, ST ANDREW'S DAY

Colin Hunter was a Victorian marine artist, born in Glasgow in 1841. More than a hundred of his paintings were exhibited at the Royal Academy Summer Exhibition in London, where the artist died in 1903. His work would have been much sought after by the aspiring middle classes when the picture that now hangs over our fireplace was purchased by my family in the 1880s.

When *Songs of Praise* recorded in the open air includes hymns with a

nautical flavour, the director has to be very imaginative if he's to stop my eyes from wandering off to Colin Hunter's picture of the herring fleet on Loch Fyne. The artist draws us into the world of a sunny afternoon in 1880. At the mouth of the small bay called the East Loch in Tarbert the fleet is tied up, so it must have been the sabbath. The autumn sun is bright enough to reflect off the roofs of the town and off the water, and there is a low mist, but a breeze is getting up and clouds are appearing in the north-west.

The weather in the Highlands, as today's tourists know, can change rapidly. In 1880, the God-fearing Presbyterians in Tarbert, had they raised their blinds and their eyes from the family Bible to see the sun, would have observed: 'It'll not last.'

Hunter's visit to Tarbert came before the handsome lantern-towered parish church overlooking the Loch had been built. The church is too small for all the paraphernalia of a traditional *Songs of Praise* and, as far as I can recall, no one has ever attempted an open-air programme there. The nearest anyone came to risking the elements was a programme in which the well-known but curiously named Toad Choir took to one of the modern Clyde ferries, singing hymns between the showers of a characteristic Scottish summer day 'doon the watter'.

PS WAVERLEY STEAMS HOME FROM TARBERT

Colin Hunter's view was almost certainly from a ferry, about to call at the pier, which still stands on the point where the herring boats in the picture are moored. In the 1880s, visitors would have arrived on the MacBrayne's steamer *Iona*. They would have been packed like sardines on the largely open deck if it was the day of the Horse Fair in July.

Just the other day we moved the picture into a brighter light, and I noticed for the first time that in one of the boats – Scottish sabbath or no sabbath – there are two fishermen at work, mending their nets.

Jesus was walking by the Sea of Galilee when he saw two brothers, Simon called Peter and his brother Andrew, casting a net into the lake; for they were fishermen. Jesus said to them, 'Come with me, and I will make you fishers of men.' At once they left their nets and followed him. Going on farther, he saw another pair of brothers, James son of Zebedee and his brother John; they were in a boat with their father Zebedee, mending their nets. He called them, and at once they left the boat and their father, and followed him.

MATTHEW 4:18–22

Strange News

● ● ● ● ● ● ● ● ● ● ● ● ●

DAYS IN ADVENT

The people that walked in darkness have seen a great light;
on those who lived in a land as dark as death
a light has dawned.

ISAIAH 9:2

For years I have been trying to photograph Durham Cathedral from the train window as I travel back and forth between Edinburgh and London on the East Coast main line. For a split second as you pass, the cathedral on the wooded hill above the River Wear appears just as it would have done to travellers centuries ago. But time after time, the results have been blurred, or obstructed by electric masts. I've tried faster film and every kind of exposure, the light has been different every time, but the result is always the same – useless.

So my hopes were high at the beginning of Advent when I had to make a stop at Durham and could get out of the train. I was sure the cathedral would be revealed in all its glory from the station. But able to stand still to take my picture for the first time, I discovered that there are wires and trees everywhere, and the entire structure is hidden as you descend the path from the station down into a deep valley.

Later in the day, after fulfilling the purpose of my visit – giving a talk to theology students about *Songs of Praise* – I was no nearer getting my photograph and it was now growing dark. I found I might just manage to get to Evensong in the cathedral if I got moving. 'There's a good short cut, a path through the woods. It's ill-lit… correction… it is not lit… but the cathedral will beckon you on, as it were.' My host told me to look first for a pasta house, and then for a little dark alley. 'Once through there, the cathedral's floodlighting will guide you,' he said confidently.

The first little dark alley I came across must have been the wrong one, because it led only to some smelly dustbins, but the next was even narrower, leading to some very dark steps. However, I kept walking because a bell had started to toll somewhere above me in the woods. Without a watch, it began to feel like a medieval pilgrimage. I was being summoned by bells.

The path really was unlit but there were steps that glimmered very faintly to prevent serious accidents. Shadowy figures were moving in the opposite direction. I pressed on.

Puffing and panting, I at last emerged out of the woods to find myself in the shadow of the great cathedral, and feel my way into the massive, dimly lit nave. At the crossing I joined a congregation of three waiting for a mid-week Advent Evensong. In front of us the medieval choir was empty, but on the left a black cassocked verger was gently tugging a long bell-rope. All that we could hear from inside was a rhythmic clunk, but his bell had guided me safely there.

When the choir appeared, it was just the altos, tenors and basses of the

lay clerks. They sang Evensong in an unaccompanied, ancient plainsong chant. It was austere and beautiful. Especially so when, as they do every night of the year, they sang the *Magnificat*.

That night the familiar words caught my imagination and it was as though I was hearing them for the first time, the story of Mary's reply to the angel who had greeted her with the news that she would give birth to the son of God, her 'Yes' to God. Christians have been singing her words for centuries but that night in the dark, almost empty cathedral, in an over-busy world of breaking headlines, it felt like strange, new, important news: 'He has filled the hungry with good things, and the rich he has sent empty away.'

I had to leave before the end of Evensong to catch the train home. Returning via the dark short cut was beyond me, so I took a circuitous route through the streets already lit by Christmas decorations. I found myself remembering a line I had recently heard in an editing suite when watching the preparations for the Advent *Songs of Praise*. It was from a song sung as part of a meditation by the blind theologian, John Hull, 'Mary, did you know that your baby boy will give sight to a blind man?'

Nearing the station, I was walking past a viewpoint beside the road, and suddenly realized that the picture of the cathedral I had been looking for was there, in front of me, glowing in the darkness. As I fiddled with my camera for the night shot, a passer-by stopped to watch me. 'Do you know,' he said, 'I've lived here for 20 years, and had never noticed that view until now?'

Tell out, my soul, the greatness of his might!
Powers and dominions lay their glory by,
Proud hearts and stubborn wills are put to flight,
The hungry fed, the humble lifted high.

TIMOTHY DUDLEY-SMITH (B. 1926)
BASED ON THE *MAGNIFICAT*

Come, Thou Long-Expected Jesus

I have very happy memories of directing *Songs of Praise* in Skipton, where a huge, enthusiastic congregation bravely fought their way through a fiendishly complicated orchestral version of 'Turn Back O Man' – I swear some of them were holding their hymn books upside down – but then they all clearly enjoyed singing this hymn in the resonant acoustic of Holy Trinity Parish Church. It is a hymn of hope for a dark day.

Come, thou long-expected Jesus,
born to set thy people free;
from our fears and sins release us;
let us find our rest in thee.

Israel's strength and consolation,
hope of all the earth thou art;
dear desire of every nation,
joy of every longing heart.

Born thy people to deliver;
born a child, and yet a king;
born to reign in us for ever;
now thy gracious kingdom bring.

By thine own eternal Spirit
rule in all our hearts alone;
by thine all-sufficient merit
raise us to thy glorious throne.

CHARLES WESLEY (1707–88)

Tales of Gloucester

SONGS OF PRAISE PREPARES FOR CHRISTMAS

In those days a decree was issued by the emperor Augustus for a census to be taken throughout the Roman world. This was the first registration of its kind; it took place when Quirinius was governor of Syria. Everyone

173

made his way to his own town to be registered. Joseph went up to Judaea from the town of Nazareth in Galilee, to register in the city of David called Bethlehem, because he was of the house of David by descent; and with him went Mary, his betrothed, who was expecting her child. While they were there the time came for her to have her baby, and she gave birth to a son, her firstborn. She wrapped him in swaddling clothes, and laid him in a manger, because there was no room for them at the inn.

LUKE 2:1–7

It was to be the most beautiful shot in the 2003 Christmas *Songs of Praise* from Gloucester Cathedral. I cannot think of any scene to surpass it in the 43 years that *Songs of Praise* has celebrated Christmas, and I hope the picture I took of the scene conveys something of its beauty. Yet at home, viewers who were not quick-eyed might easily have missed it, for it lasted less than two seconds. While the cathedral choir sang the line in the second verse of 'Once in royal David's city', beginning 'He came down to earth from heaven', camera 3, guided by director Norman Ivison, flashed a fleeting evocation of heaven in front of our eyes. For the Dean and Chapter and the entire cathedral choir down on earth, those two seconds were the result of a whole hour's choreography, and many hours' rehearsal.

It was simple, said the BBC director. All they had to do was to walk very slowly in a straight line down a dark corridor towards a very bright light.

Anyone who has been to a cathedral and watched the choir procession at the beginning and end of worship may have noticed that they appear to glide. My own interest in how this would go on *Songs of Praise* was because Liz and I had tried this ourselves at Gloucester, one Whitsunday when the choir had led the congregation around the whole cathedral as we sang the processional hymn 'Hail thee, festival day'. As the professionals glided elegantly on ahead, we had swayed and stumbled along behind them. It is, I suspect, a distinctly Church of England Chapter skill, to be able to look holy and not fall over in procession.

For his grand opening moments, Norman Ivison had chosen the beautiful cloisters of the cathedral, built in the 1350s and containing the earliest surviving fan vaulting. (The cloisters, incidentally, are also a place of pilgrimage for Harry Potter fans, transformed for the films into a part of Hogwarts School.)

The atmosphere for making *Songs of Praise* is somewhat less dramatic, but there was enough mystery for the Dean, his Chapter and the choir, as Dave Brazier, the floor manager, gently coaxed the verger, the crucifer who carried the huge processional cross, and two servers carrying tall, lit candles to edge forwards slowly and almost imperceptibly towards a light that was blinding them like an undipped car headlamp beside the camera. Now and again an encouraging comment came from the invisible cameraman behind it. The director's voice was an indistinct squeak through headphones as he worked with the floor manager to turn the shot into what the *Songs of Praise* team likes to call 'magic'.

While I watched them rehearse and remembered how fast a director has to work things out as he looks at his bank of TV monitors to achieve the result he wants, in what to choir and clergy will seem like an eternity, there was plenty of time for me to wander off to think about the tales of Gloucester that I had been hearing on this late autumn afternoon.

Earlier that day I had met Richard Cann, who was carrying the processional cross for 'the shot'. BBC equipment had blocked the door to the tall Victorian cupboard where he keeps the cross. As I helped him heave the equipment clear, Richard told me that he has been involved with the cathedral since the 1940s, when he was a chorister singing under the legendary Dr Herbert Sumsion. He sang in the famous Three Choirs Festival (Gloucester, Hereford and Worcester), took part in the first performance of Herbert Howells's 'Hymnus Paradisi' and even sang for Ralph Vaughan Williams.

His memories gave me a vivid portrait of life in the cathedral. There in the nave I could picture Vaughan Williams and Herbert Howells, composers of hymn tunes and music that for so many people express the soul of England. In extreme old age, Vaughan Williams had kept going magnificently, and musicians sang and played for him even when his conductor's beat became uncertain. Today, Richard Cann's youngest son is a lay clerk in the choir of

Norwich Cathedral, and his family will soon have taken part in nearly a century of church music.

In the gloom, when the TV lights had gone out after the first rehearsal, I had found Olive Withycombe attending faithfully to 'Bishop Ellicott', as she does once a fortnight. Olive ('I'm a Gloucester girl!' she announced with pride.) is one of the volunteer cleaners and a member of the cathedral 'welcome' team. With another friend, she looks after the tomb of the former bishop of Gloucester, who died in 1905.

When I found her, she was sponging the marble effigy very gently, but she revealed that a little furniture polish is also permitted now and again, which explains why the tomb shines even on a dark day.

'Of course,' said Olive as she worked on, 'he's not here.'

'No,' I agreed, rather pleased that our conversation had moved on to theology. Olive paused in her sponging, took a step back and said, 'No. He's in Birchington.'

Once again, the cathedral's history had come unexpectedly alive as Olive told me how the bishop's remains, like another great Victorian, the artist Danté Gabriel Rossetti, awaits the resurrection in a small churchyard in faraway Kent.

In the Lady Chapel under the great east window, the largest medieval window in Europe, I had already sat down at the back before I noticed a row of women in front of me, sitting together facing the altar. They were taking turns to pray aloud, but not very aloud. I could scarcely make out their words, but every so often there would be a fervent 'Amen'. It seemed right to respect their space and stay at the back, but the quiet prayers made me look first at the altar cross and then at the huge stone screen behind it.

It was a shock to realize that the stone was scarred and bruised and that I was looking at 18 empty niches. It must have taken very determined efforts by Oliver Cromwell's soldiers, who came into the cathedral in the seventeenth century, to destroy all the ancient statues that had once meant so much to Christians in Gloucester. And then I realized that the women praying in front of so much damage were praying for the people of Iraq, Afghanistan and the Balkans, where men still smash holy places. My cathedral guidebook says that there are modern tapestries in the niches, but it almost seems better that they are removed – until their prayers and ours are answered.

As they gathered their bags, I talked to them and found that they were members of the Mothers' Union from a distant part of the diocese of Gloucester. They hadn't come just for Christmas shopping and, like Richard and Olive, were at home whenever they came to the cathedral.

I lit a candle before I left, attracted by some words displayed underneath the ranks of tiny lights lit by passing strangers and the cathedral family:

Lighting a candle is a prayer
When we have gone, it stays alight
Kindling in the hearts and minds of others
The prayers we have already offered for them and for others
For the sad, the sick, the suffering
And prayers of thankfulness too.

Lighting a candle is a parable
Burning itself out, it gives light to others.
Christ gave himself for others.
He calls us to give ourselves.

Lighting a candle is a symbol
Of love and hope, of light and warmth
Our world needs them all.

Back in the cloister, the choristers' candles were burning down and they were still there, practising their slow procession, moving at the speed of a glacier, more or less to the satisfaction of the director.

'It could all be better,' said the invisible voices. 'Then it will be quite good,' added Norman, who does not go in for superlatives. The procession then had to perform yet another exotic move, walking backwards away from the camera and the light.

I had not got the nerve to discover what the Dean of Gloucester, the Very Reverend Nick Bury, who was right up against the wall at the end of the

cloister, was making of it all, but he emerged with a look of quiet triumph after the final manoeuvre had been performed flawlessly. He deserved to be proud of his team. It may have been just another day in the life of the cathedral, but in the end the shot looked wonderful, and it deserved more than a couple of seconds on *Songs of Praise*.

Later that night, the cathedral nave was full, with everyone in the congregation holding candles while they sang the Christmas story in familiar hymns and carols. A platoon of vergers led by Nicholas Hilyer performed 'ducking and diving' miracles as guttering candles here, there and everywhere were replaced without their manoeuvres being seen on camera. Aled Jones did his star turn, welcoming viewers in front of a huge Christmas tree and then, to the evident delight of the united choir, joined them to sing carols for the whole evening.

If the choir and clergy had wondered what they had let themselves in for after their slow-motion ballet in the cloisters, in the evening the atmosphere changed completely, and the teamwork of the people of the city of Gloucester together with all the cathedral staff and the BBC was worthy of an award. The evening ended with the dean's Christmas blessing:

May the songs of the angels
The eagerness of the shepherds
The perseverance of the wise men
The obedience of Joseph and Mary
And the joy of the Christ child
Be in your hearts this Christmas.

BC:AD

● ● ● ● ● ● ● ● ● ● ● ● ● ●

23 DECEMBER

Lord, now lettest thou thy servant depart in peace,
According to thy word:
For mine eyes have seen thy salvation,
Which thou hast prepared before the face of all people;
A light to lighten the Gentiles, and the glory of thy
   people Israel.

LUKE 2:29–32

It may not be merely far-fetched, but plain silly, even possibly blasphemous, to compare our bleary-eyed old dog, MacBean, with saintly old Simeon from Luke's Gospel. Nevertheless, I find the ancient words said or sung every night at Evensong in Anglican cathedrals running round my head.

MacBean is very old. How very old we will never know for sure. When we chose him at the Edinburgh dogs and cats' home two years ago, all we knew about this collie-cross was the name on his cage – MacBean – and that he had been picked up after Christmas, wandering the streets in the neighbouring county; everything else is a mystery. We would love to know how he came to be lost. Once in Edinburgh, I thought I had found a clue when I bought the *Big Issue* from a man in Princes Street, or more precisely from his dog, a dead ringer for MacBean. 'This is Deadly,' the vendor told me when I asked, 'and I think he's about fourteen.' As I handed over the money, Deadly gave me a steady stare before he went back to sleep with a heavy sigh. So like MacBean. When I reported all this back to Liz, we both agreed that we could easily imagine MacBean selling the *Big Issue* before he came to us.

The relationship between human and dog can be very close, and a recent newspaper article illustrates the lengths some people are prepared to go to in order to have a conversation with their pet. Scientists in Japan, I read, have developed a miniature computer, which your dog wears on his collar, and the programme analyses the barking and then translates it into the spoken word. As you might expect, the Japanese scientists found that there were a lot of 'let me in' and 'let me out' commands as well as frequent calls for food and walks, but what made me believe that they really might be on to something was their claim that by far the most frequent thing their dogs were saying was: 'Look at me!' But this wouldn't be enough to tell us where MacBean came from.

Another reason that it would be wasted on us is that, apart from in dire emergency, MacBean rarely barks. It was the first thing I noticed about him. It was like bedlam at the dogs and cats' home on the day Liz and I went in search of a puppy to adopt, everyone barking furiously as we passed along the cages of the pound. It was quiet only at the far end of the passage and here, under his nameplate, quite silent but immediately making firm eye contact with me, was MacBean. I knew at once, although his puppy days were quite obviously in the far distant past, he would be coming home with us.

At home, he has always seemed to be happiest lying on the carpet facing the glass inner front door, one cocked ear and one eye monitoring proceedings in our house behind him, while keeping his other eye intent on passers-by. He has never barked at people coming to the door, although he does fire off a warning volley if he sees another dog go by. He has also learned to tell us about his immediate needs with a few short commands – which we haven't needed any computerized collar to translate.

Today he is at his usual post. Increasingly, his eyes are fixed on that door as if he is waiting for someone. Since he first arrived we have often thought that he still has hopes of his original owner turning up, and we have even wondered if they were perhaps separated by death. Some sweet old lady, perhaps, who spoiled him. On the other hand, MacBean reserves his greatest interest for anyone who arrives wearing jeans that are past their best, so that sends us back to the *Big Issue* idea.

In these last few days of Advent, MacBean has become almost completely silent. He still looks at us a lot, his eyes affectionate but bleary due to cataracts. It reminds me of a couplet that long ago my father used to recite to cheer up our short-sighted household:

Mine eyes are dim, I cannot see –
I have not brought my specs with me!

Until a few days ago, MacBean was a friendly if somewhat lugubrious companion, not beyond occasional outbursts of spontaneous cheerfulness, particularly in anticipation of a walk, and often at inconvenient moments. Just a week ago, he decided to push his way to a secret hiding place under the table where the Christmas crib is set up, empty still, of course, except for its regular occupants of sheep, ox and ass. As MacBean rolled over on his side to get more comfortable, he got tangled up with the tablecloth, pulling the stable with the empty manger and all the animals down on top of himself. He reappeared covered in bits of straw, a bit shocked, but unhurt and wagging his tail with surprise at his own cleverness. The good outcome was that we now knew that a similar incident, when we had come downstairs a morning or two earlier to find sheep, oxen, three-legged donkey and straw all over the carpet, was not, as we had assumed, young Toby the cat's doing.

Seeing MacBean covered in the contents of our crib made me think of a Beatrix Potter story, *The Tailor of Gloucester*, which describes the night before Christmas when all the animals were able to talk – a legend perhaps based on the 'Mass in Gallicantu' (Mass at Cockcrow), an ancient pre-Reformation Service from the Sarum prayer book. An ancient painting in St Mary's Iffley, near Oxford, also appears to depict just such a moment. I thought, if ever MacBean is to tell us his story, it will be now.

But in these last few days before Christmas night, MacBean's area of interest is diminishing rapidly. The crib is safe from him now. He hardly moves from his post in the hall by the front door. The sad thought strikes us that this old dog may not be celebrating the birth of Christ in our company this year. Increasingly, his eyes are fixed on that door as if he is waiting for someone. Anyone who has been close to a beloved old animal will recognize this moment. MacBean is clean and tidy and patient and good, but he seems to be telling us that he has had enough of this world.

This morning, as the 'postie' rushes up the street delivering last Christmas cards, I come down to an unusually silent hall. Has MacBean slipped away in his sleep? I don't know if that is my prayer for him, or my hope for myself that we won't have to live with making a decision for him. But he is still here, quietly awake.

For two days now he hasn't eaten, which means he hasn't had his arthritis pain-killing tablets even when hidden in his favourite food. Liz decides to buy him some best fillet steak. MacBean does not even give a cursory sniff at our offering. He looks at us sadly, then turns back to face the door.

What is going on in his head? Is he perhaps waiting for his old owner to come and take him home? I must face the fact that we shall never know. Neither Japanese computer nor ancient Christian legend is going to give him the magical power to talk. But in the language we *have* learned to understand, from loving him for two years, everything about him tells us now that he wants to leave us, and needs our help to make this happen.

This afternoon, MacBean does not look up when the vet comes into the hall. A week ago he had bounced into her surgery for his regular check-up. A week ago he was still making a regular inspection of his village message posts, his familiar lopsided limp, perhaps a bit more pronounced, still making people laugh, the oldest dog on the block still with tricks to play. Now our dear collie-cross is calm and quiet as life swiftly ebbs out of him. If nothing else, it is a parting gift to us in our grief that he dies so peacefully as we sit on the floor beside him and stroke his fur. When his heart stops beating at last, the vet closes the eyes still fixed on the doorway to the street outside.

Now it is evening. MacBean has passed from 'is' to 'was'. Nothing better describes that moment when MacBean finally left us than the two lines that end one of U.A. Fanthorpe's Christmas poems, BC:AD, because like her 'three members of an obscure Persian sect', MacBean has surely

Walked haphazard by starlight straight
Into the kingdom of heaven.

And the words of Simeon are still running round my head.

'Lord, now lettest thou thy servant depart in
peace according to thy word.'

Just a few weeks ago, at the very beginning of Advent, I was standing in Durham Cathedral as the choir chanted these words. I was remembering then how on this very spot I had produced the hymns for a *Songs of Praise*'s survey of Christian faith in the last decade of the twentieth century, a programme which had somehow revealed so much of the muddle and messiness of faith. As the *Songs of Praise* congregation had sung hymns for the Christian year, we had heard stories of many personal, often unorthodox, experiences of faith – moments of truth in unexpected events. Even though many of us can't seem to help turning into Doubting Thomases, we still long to believe that a forgiving, death-defying God is amongst us, and how sometimes, just for a second, we know that he is.

And at Evensong in Durham this Advent, I was also remembering Harry Secombe making a Christmas *Highway* here, under bright TV lights in the chancel. His star guest that evening, the world-famous opera singer, Jessye Norman, sang like an angel, but she couldn't quite respond to the great man's natural courtesy and irrepressible humour on her only visit to the cathedral. I hope the light of the world shone through in the final programme, but as always there had been much muddle and mess and it had sometimes felt more of a televisual than an Advent experience of waiting.

In all Sir Harry's *Highways*, and *Songs of Praise* over two decades, allowing his audiences to join him on his own quest for faith, I believe he, too, was like Old Simeon in Luke's Gospel. By the time his life ended, he had been able to show us what he had seen, and that he was grateful to his maker. His work was done because, in countless interviews and songs, he had shared with us a glimpse of what is to come.

The news is spreading round the village that MacBean has died, 'Oh, no! Not MacBean,' called different voices from all over the Mini-mart when Liz went across the road for something, and had to answer the usual question: How's MacBean today? There will be sad faces whenever the news is heard around the village this Christmas. He never chose to roam in the wide open spaces, always preferring to go wherever he could find people. Rushing up to greet total strangers, he soon made friends with everyone in the village. Teenagers, elderly widows, men in vans delivering things, gardeners, kids going to and from school – everyone was soon greeting MacBean by name. On his maddening, inconvenient, whatever-the-weather walks through our community, he was our ambassador. People we had never spoken to even after nearly ten years living here now know our names and we know theirs. I hope MacBean found a little geriatric contentment in changing our lives so much for the better.

We are waiting for that moment when we, with millions around the world, celebrate a birth in the stable 2,000 years ago. Liz is very strict with our Christmas crib: the star and a few angels seem to be hovering about already, but I know the plaster figures of Mary and Joseph and the baby will not appear in the straw until midnight Christmas Eve, the shepherds won't arrive until Christmas morning and the three wise men are not allowed to put in an appearance until a day or two later.

And in 40 short days it will be Candlemas. Old Simeon's prayer will be read again at the morning Eucharist. But, as we used to say after childhood visits to the News Cinemas, 'This is where we came in.'

I must get up and go out now, for a last walk in the evening light, which each day will last a little longer now. We plan to scatter MacBean's ashes round the garden in the New Year that awaits us. There will be new strangers to become friends, old memories to talk of again and, somewhere in the middle, *Songs of Praise* bringing us stories of people's lives that will shed new light on an old story.

BC:AD

This was the moment when Before
Turned into After, and the future's
Uninvented timekeepers presented arms.

This was the moment when nothing
Happened. Only dull peace
Sprawled boringly over the earth.

This was the moment when even energetic Romans
Could find nothing better to do
Than counting heads in remote provinces.

And this was the moment
When a few farm workers and three
Members of an obscure Persian sect

Walked haphazard by starlight straight
Into the kingdom of heaven.

U.A. FANTHORPE (B. 1929)

Joy to the World!

25 DECEMBER

Joy to the world, the Lord has come!
Let earth receive her King;
let every heart prepare him room,
and heaven and nature sing,
and heaven and nature sing,
and heaven, and heaven and nature sing.

ISAAC WATTS (1673–1748) ALTD

What a Prospect!

31 DECEMBER

How silently, how silently,
the wondrous gift is given!
So God imparts to human hearts
the blessings of his heaven.
No ear may hear his coming;
but in this world of sin,
where meek souls will receive him, still
the dear Christ enters in.

PHILLIPS BROOKS (1835–93) ALTD

The old year ended apocalyptically, with the sudden disappearance of our garden. 'What a prospect!' exclaimed an elderly relative, as we sat down for a family New Year's Eve lunch of Christmas leftovers. 'What a prospect!'

she repeated, peering out of the dining room window to where the garden should have been, in a tone more appropriate to a biblical prophecy of doom.

'The prospect' was indeed bleak. A wall of snow falling in tightly packed flakes meant only one thing: our family, with our visiting relatives, would be trapped in a post-Christmas time warp until the thaw. Our garden, the place of childhood magical adventures and still, in student days, big enough for secret hiding places to make a welcome sanctuary out of earshot of relatives at war in the house, had vanished under a blanket of snow. A deadening silence had replaced the sounds of traffic on the nearby main road, and gloomy estimates from the great aunts, before the outer front door was closed plunging the hallway into darkness, were that it was already a foot deep.

'And more to come,' said my grandmother with the little chuckle which always marked her grimmer predictions.

Grandmother had, as usual, awoken us all that morning with the noise of the 'Home Service' blaring from her radio. Her day's radio listening always began with *Lift Up Your Hearts*, an old-fashioned and far more pious equivalent of today's *Thought for the Day*. Then followed the weather forecast from London, read out at what today would seem like dictation speed and full of mysteries like 'occluded fronts', 'troughs' and 'anti-cyclones'. My grandmother was an expert at interpreting these prognostications, somehow relating them to the dire events that had befallen the people of the Old Testament featured in *Lift Up Your Hearts*. That day 'the man' had announced 'snow warning' before the sound of the 'pips' marked eight o'clock and she had set her watch for another day of monitoring the chronically unpunctual activities of my brother and myself.

Unfortunately Grandmother was right this time. More was to come. Our white-out blizzard in the last hours of 1962 was to be the beginning of long months of snow in early 1963.

Our garden often looked its best on a winter morning. Hearing the blackbirds looking for berries in the climbing pyrocanthus outside my bedroom, I would look out across the lawn and over our summerhouse, which perversely faced

north, to two huge trees. My favourite was a tall English elm, which has still, I think or hope, survived decades of the terrible tree plague, Dutch Elm disease. Both trees were survivors of a copse forming the edge of an eighteenth-century estate, and there were other more intriguing remnants of that once-grand property in our garden.

What had always fascinated me was the mystery of the hundreds of tons of fine, white Bath Portland stone that lay around our garden. On winter mornings they were often coated with sparkling hoar frost. Here and there were carefully carved lumps of a stone from underground quarries more than a hundred miles away and there were many flagstones, which had been laid to create a network of wide paths, edged with fine blocks, while in a far corner there was a massive pile, which we imagined had once kept eighteenth-century convicts busy. My brother and I used to clamber precariously to the top of the heap, wielding a sledgehammer to see if we could find fossils. It was like a jigsaw puzzle begun by a giant, but abandoned after only the edges had been completed.

My school friend, Christopher, after evenings of singing in Westminster Abbey in the special choir, was convinced that it was at least part, if not all, of a ruined church. So we tried to match pieces together, lugging them around the garden until our old wooden wheelbarrow collapsed under the weight. If we turned over the right flagstones, would we find names carved in Latin on the underside?

Alas, we did not possess the skills of television's *Time Team*, and our detective work was not even up to the standards of *Children's Hour*'s heroic boy detectives, Norman and Henry Bones. As we lurked behind the hedges and fences of neighbouring gardens, it was clear that the mystery stones were only to be found in our garden. Nearby Shortlands House, built in 1702, was completely intact, and the church of St Mary's in Shortlands, a Victorian Kentish ragstone building shattered by bombing, lay in ruins not far away. Could our garden be filled with bits and pieces of the old fourteenth-century parish church in Beckenham, rebuilt in the 1880s into the present St George's and nowadays scene of regular broadcasts, including *Songs of Praise*? That, too, I now realize, must have been built of local ragstone.

The deep snow of that winter covered our mystery white stones for almost three months, and was to be the end of long, carefree childhood days spent in the garden. Soon afterwards a BBC career would mean that there was only time for an occasional dash through the orchard with a motor mower, crashing into the stones still lying around the lawn. With the death of my mother in 1973, after a last sun-filled summer in the garden, it was time to leave our family home forever. Our old orchard was replaced by an executive home, complete with its own swimming pool. The stones vanished.

During that long post-Christmas period, while walled in with snow and relatives, I passed the time by tape recording family life and conversation, first as a joke and then because I realized that by diverting the elders from scrapping with each other into their memories of Victorian England, we could all escape from boredom. I still have the taped memories of early cars preceded by men carrying red flags, of meeting the composer Edward Elgar, and a long story about a famous surgeon, James Scott of Bromley, who a century earlier would have been our neighbour. His secret remedies, dressings applied to diseased joints and ulcerated legs, were so successful that the sick who endured long journeys to see him left their crutches behind. In 1824, an anonymous admirer wrote a ballad about Scott's work:

See them, on first arriving crawl,
And limp and tumble down;
But in a fortnight, one and all
Go skipping round the town.

Though past belief, 'tis yet a truth
I'm now about to speak –
He can bring back the bloom of youth
Upon the faded cheek!

Scott retired in 1829, but still saw patients at his home until he died in the winter of 1848. His gardens have long been replaced with neat villas, and nearby ponds and springs, once thought to have healing properties, have also vanished. I have recently rediscovered, amongst old family treasures, a detailed nineteenth-century plan that was mentioned, including Dr Scott's garden, which shows paths from all directions to a spot marked 'old grotto'. We should have realized then, as we ate our New Year lunch, that the secret of our stones lay in the very story about Dr Scott that we were all listening to my great aunt tell, and I was recording.

While helping recently with a small organization in Bosnia, where Christians and Moslems are working together to rebuild churches and mosques destroyed in the civil war of the 1990s, the elegant stones of one of Europe's most historic mosques have been found. They were buried under many tons of waste and rubbish, and rediscovered only as a result of stories about what had happened to them emerging as trust was re-established. Skilled architects and engineers now plan to reassemble this formidable stone jigsaw into a place of reconciliation between people of different faiths, once at war with each other and now neighbours in the developing story of Europe.

At the dawn of 1963, our old stones were buried under feet of fresh snow. 'What a prospect!' said a gloomy great aunt. What a prospect – if we did indeed grow up in the shade of the old elm in a garden with magical properties made by the scattered old stones of a grotto that had once belonged to a healer.

Then the angel showed me the river of the water of life, sparkling like crystal, flowing from the throne of God and of the Lamb down the middle of the city's street. On either side of the river stood a tree of life, which yields twelve crops of fruit, one for each month of the year. The leaves of the trees are for the healing of the nations. Every accursed thing shall disappear. The throne of God and of the Lamb will be there, and his servants shall worship him; they shall see him face to face and bear his name on their foreheads. There shall be no more night, nor will they need the light of lamp or sun, for the Lord God will give them light; and they shall reign for ever.
REVELATION 22:1–5

The following hymn was introduced to *Songs of Praise* in a programme looking to the future in Belfast, when life was particularly difficult. It also makes an excellent New Year resolution:

Let peace begin with me,
let this be the moment now;
with every step I take,
let this be my solemn vow:
to take each moment and live each moment
in peace eternally.
Let there be peace on earth
and let it begin with me.
SY MILLER AND JILL JACKSON